CRYSTAL PALACE
SPEEDWAY

CRYSTAL PALACE
SPEEDWAY
A HISTORY OF THE GLAZIERS

NORMAN JACOBS

FONTHILL

Frontispiece: An aerial view of the Crystal Palace and grounds.

Fonthill Media Limited
www.fonthillmedia.com
office@fonthillmedia.com

Published in the United Kingdom 2012

British Library Cataloguing in Publication Data:
A catalogue record for this book is available from the
British Library

ISBN: 978-1-78155-062-5 (print)
ISBN: 978-1-78155-156-1 (e-book)

Typeset in 11/13 pt Sabon LT Std
Printed and bound in England

Connect with us
 facebook.com/fonthillmedia twitter.com/fonthillmedia

Contents

Acknowledgements

As always, I have relied heavily on Peter Jackson for the statistics. I would also like to thank John Hyam and Terry Stone for pointing me in the direction of useful material and Triss and Brian Sharp, sons of Crystal Palace's first captain, for talking to me at length and showing me their father's memorabilia.

Photographs used in the book come from a variety of sources and I would like to thank the following for allowing me to use theirs: Ian Moultray, Mike Hunter and the Friends of Edinburgh Speedway, Mike Kemp, John Chaplin, Martin Appleby, Tom Marriott, Brian Darby, Triss and Brian Sharp, Nigel Bird and John Skinner of http://www.defunctspeedway.co.uk.

Last, but my no means least, I would like to thank my wife, Linda, for all her help with getting the photographs ready for publication.

Introduction

The original Crystal Palace was built in 1851 in Hyde Park, London, by the architect Joseph Paxton to house the Great Exhibition, the brainchild of Queen Victoria's husband, Prince Albert. The palace was a masterpiece of engineering, built entirely of glass and iron; it was itself the main exhibit among more than 14,000 examples of the most up-to-date modern technology from around the world.

The exhibition lasted for six months and attracted visitors from all over Great Britain and the world. On its closure, it was agreed that the Crystal Palace had to be preserved, and so it was moved to a permanent home in South London at Sydenham Hill. The opportunity was taken to modify and enlarge the building while at the same time surrounding it with parklands, which included gardens, fountains, terraces and cascades. Among the attractions in the parklands was the first-ever dinosaur exhibition.

A football stadium and a sports ground were built in the parklands and many FA Cup finals in the early years of the competition were held there, the last of which was in 1914, when George V became the first reigning monarch to watch the final. Even before the creation of the present day Crystal Palace F.C., a team bearing the name Crystal Palace played in the competition, its players coming from the staff of the Crystal Palace itself. For a few years, top class club cricket was also played in the park by the London County Cricket Club.

Ever on the look-out for more attractions to entice the paying customers, the trustees hit on the idea of introducing motorcycle racing around the grounds. A mile-long circuit was marked out on the gravel pathways, and with the support of the Streatham and Sydenham motorcycle clubs, path racing commenced in 1926 under the management of Fred Mockford and

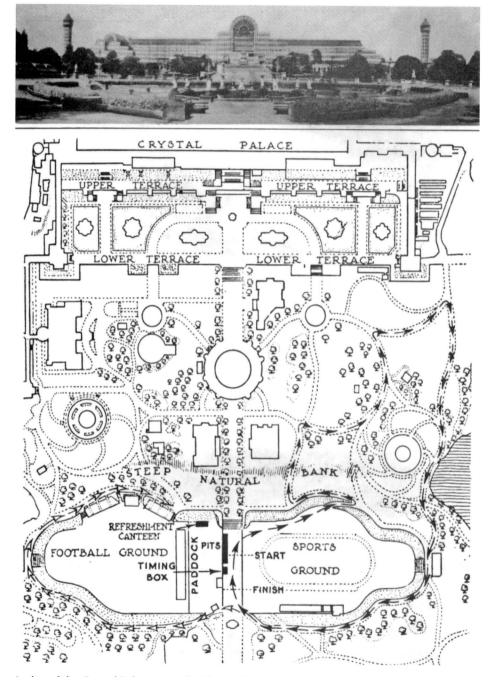

A plan of the Crystal Palace grounds. The track later occupied the site of the football ground shown in the bottom left-hand corner. The black arrows indicate the path racing circuit.

Cecil Smith. Riders at these early meetings included Triss Sharp, Gus Kuhn, Joe Francis and one of the men who was to be intimately involved in bringing speedway to this country, Lionel Wills.

Wills visited Australia later in 1926 where he saw an advertisement in a Sydney newspaper for a speedway meeting. Not really knowing what speedway was, he went along to see what it was all about. He couldn't believe his eyes when he saw motorcycles without brakes broadsiding around a relatively small oval circuit at fantastic speeds. There was nothing like this back in Britain and he was quick to recognise that this new sport could be a real money spinner. He immediately set about writing articles for the motorcycle press in his home country, extolling the virtues of this new form of motorcycle racing. It was the age of speed, and watching these latter-day gladiators hurtling round the track at impossible angles, spraying flying cinders behind them, handlebars almost touching and seemingly on the verge of crashing at every corner, sent a thrill through even the most hardened spectators. It was new, electrifying, and everyone wanted to see it.

Wills was followed by a number of other British visitors, among whom were Captain Olliver, Captain Mallins and Stanley Glanfield. They were each so enthused by this new sport that they too sent reports back to this country in the most enthusiastic terms.

Lionel Wills returned to Britain in around October 1927, and his first port of call was his path racing home of Crystal Palace. There he had a meeting with Fred Mockford and Cecil Smith where he tried to convince them that speedway would be an attractive crowd pleaser. He showed them a rough drawing of his proposed track, which was a third of a mile long, similar to the track he had seen at Sydney. Wills advised Mockford and Smith to contact the Sydney promoter, Johnnie Hoskins, who had told him that he was interested in promoting speedway in the United Kingdom. Ever the astute businessmen, they saw the potential in this new sport and cabled Hoskins straight away.

Hoskins advised shortening the length of Wills' track and Mockford and Smith took his advice, converting the old football pitch into a 440-yard-long dirt track, 33 feet wide on the straights and 55 feet wide on the bends. The track was banked 1 in 20 at both ends, with a riding surface consisting of several inches of finely graded cinders. The safety fence was made of sprung wire netting and was 4 feet high on the outside edge of the track, behind which there was some 6 feet of no man's land and then a 4-foot iron railing fence. There was seating accommodation for 8,000 people and stepped standing accommodation for a further 65,000. The cost of the conversion was £5,000.

Freddie Mockford and Cecil Smith, the two men responsible for bringing speedway to Crystal Palace in 1928.

The vivid descriptions sent back by Wills and the others had caught the attention of not only motorcyclists in general, but more importantly, promoters like Mockford and Smith, willing to try to stage similar events in Great Britain. As a result, there were a number of attempts made to replicate the Australian speedway tracks, firstly at Camberley on 7 May 1927 and then at Droylsden on 25 June 1927. But it was the meeting at High Beech on 19 February 1928 that was to go down in history as the first serious attempt to introduce speedway into Great Britain, though even this was not really speedway as we know it today; the Auto Cycle Union (A.C.U.) rules stated that all bikes must have rear wheel brakes and riders were not allowed to put their foot down on the track. Lionel Wills and Stanley Glanfield were both involved in the planning and organisation of the meeting, and with some 20-30,000 spectators turning up and the meeting making front page headlines in the national newspapers, the new sport quickly caught the imagination of the public; tracks began to spring up all over Great Britain. By April, the A.C.U. had relaxed its rules and speedway as it had been seen in Australia and as we understand it today had well and truly arrived.

On 10 April 1928, a large party of top Australian riders under the two leading promoters of the day left Australia on board the SS *Oronsay* to show the Britons how this new sport should be done. Among them were Vic

An aerial view of the track under construction.

Huxley, Frank Arthur, Frank Pearce, Charlie Spinks and Dick Smythe under their promoter, A. J. Hunting. Johnnie Hoskins also accompanied his riders, Ron Johnson, Charlie Datson and Sig Schlam.

Although there had been no specific arrangement made beforehand, Hoskins immediately made for Crystal Palace with his three riders to help Mockford and Smith organise their first meeting.

The first major track to open in London was Stamford Bridge on 5 May 1928. Just two weeks later, on 19 May, Crystal Palace opened its doors to the new sport for the first time.

Chapter One

The 1920s

1928

Crystal Palace's opening announcement placed in *The Motor Cycle* magazine of 17 May 1928 said that the chief event of the first meeting would be a match race between England and Australia for £100. Representing England were to be Roger Frogley, Les Blakeborough and Colin Watson, while Australia's team was to consist of Hoskins' three riders: Johnson, Datson and Schlam. Admission prices were 1s 6d (7½p) with free parking for motor cycles and cars. Stand seats were 2s (10p) and 5s (25p).

When the big day came the heavens opened and for about an hour before the start of the meeting there was a steady downpour. In spite of this, the public swarmed into the grounds and by the advertised starting time of 3.30 p.m., all the seats were taken with thousands more standing. Because of the rain and the need to treat the track, it was announced that the start would be postponed for half an hour. It was reported that the crowd 'bore the discomfort with great patience'. Not only did they have to put up with the rain, but the loud speakers broke down and all announcements were made by megaphone from the centre green. Once the meeting got started, the amount of water on the track caused it to become terribly rutted, necessitating a short interval during the racing to allow a 10-ton steamroller to go round flattening it out.

The meeting got underway with a 1-mile (four-lap) scratch race between C. N. Deller on his Cotton Blackburne, Les Blakeborough on his Cotton and J. G. Langman and H. W. Sallis, both riding AJSs. The race was won by Blakeborough from Langman. The next event, another 1-mile scratch race, was won by rising English star, Roger Frogley.

The programme for Crystal Palace's first meeting on 19 May 1928, featuring the 'Great International Match' between England and Australia.

The main event of the day – the match between England and Australia – followed; it was to involve three individual match races with slightly different teams to those advertised in *The Motor Cycle*. The first heat saw Lionel Wills take on Ron Johnson, riding a 345 Harley Davidson Peashooter. As the race started it became apparent that Johnson's Peashooter lacked the power of Wills' 499 Rudge Whitworth. Nevertheless, Johnson's greater experience saw him get a good start and stay in front of the Englishman, taking the outside while Wills stuck to the white line. However, Wills' machine was clearly much faster down the straights and on lap three, Johnson's machine missed several beats, giving Wills the chance to draw level. Johnson's bike continued to misfire on the last lap and Wills was able to take him on the inside and forge ahead, eventually winning by 15 yards. The crowd went wild as the more experienced Australians had been expected to win all three races.

In heat two, Sig Schlam, the holder of the Australian 350cc Championship, took on Les Blakeborough. This time the bikes were more evenly matched; Schlam was mounted on a 345 Harley Davidson while Blakeborough rode a 348 Cotton. Unfortunately, Blakeborough suffered engine failure on lap two. Schlam then put on a wonderful exhibition of broadsiding for the spectators, but on the last lap his Harley suddenly let out an enormous 'scream' and died; he was forced to push home to even up the match score.

The third and deciding heat brought together Roger Frogley on his 499 Rudge Whitworth and Charlie Datson, the holder of the World 500cc half-mile dirt track record, on his 494 Douglas. So far both of the other Australians, Johnson and Schlam, had experienced mechanical problems, and it looked as though Datson would be no exception as he had trouble getting his bike started. Eventually the heat got underway, though it was clear that there was something very wrong with the Douglas as smoke poured from the machine for two laps, by which time Frogley was a quarter of a lap ahead. Suddenly, Datson's machine seemed to recover, and he put in a hair-raising lap to catch the Englishman. His cornering held the crowd spellbound as he hurled his Douglas round the bends, sending up a bow wave of wet cinders nearly twice as high as himself, but he couldn't manage to get past Frogley, who came across the finishing line just a few feet in front. England won 2-1 over Australia in what could be said to be the first international, albeit very unofficial, between the two countries.

The deciding race for the £100 prize between the three victors followed. Once again, Schlam's bike played up and there was one false rolling start as he dropped too far behind the others. At the second time of asking, however, the three of them got away together. There was a three-way dead heat into

One of Crystal Palace's pioneering Australians, Charlie Datson.

Arthur Willimot, who rode for Crystal Palace in 1929.

the first bend, but Schlam's experience showed and he was into his broadside like lightning, coming out on to the back straight with a substantial lead, but once again, his motor cut out and he was forced to retire. Frogley won the battle of the two Englishmen, walking off with the £100 prize. The *Speedway News'* summary of the International event was that 'less experienced riders on the more reliable machines ruled the day.'

The meeting continued with further scratch races and handicap events with Frogley, Wills and Blakeborough continuing to win most of the events. One other English rider who took part in a couple of the events was Arthur Willimot.

Although the international had been a bit of a disappointment because of the Australians' mechanical problems, Mockford, Smith, Hoskins and Wills were very pleased with the crowd's reactions and decided to continue holding speedway meetings every Saturday afternoon until the end of the season. The local newspaper, the *South London Press*, was obviously very impressed. Summing up the meeting, their reporter said, 'The new sport of broadsiding made its debut at the Crystal Palace on Saturday when dirt track racing was introduced for the first time. A hectic afternoon provided a variety of new positions unknown either to Mr Euclid or Epstein.'

The following week saw the three Australians return, along with Frogley, Wills and Blakeborough, to take part in a series of scratch races, handicap races and match races, but once again, the Australians were disappointing as both Datson and Schlam suffered further mechanical problems. Once more, Frogley proved himself to be the best of the home bunch, beating Datson in a match race and winning the 1-mile scratch race final.

On 2 June a 'Big Six' event was held. This was run as a series of three match races with the three winners going into a grand final. The first heat saw Arthur Willimot beat Ron Johnson, the Australian suffering the usual mechanical problems. Wills and Schlam came together for the second heat, with Wills taking the inside line and Schlam showering the crowd with cinders as he rode round the fence to win. Heat three saw the third race in as many weeks between Frogley and Datson. Once again, Datson's engine packed up on the second lap, but Frogley sportingly stopped and offered a re-run. Frogley shot off into the lead at the start of the second attempt, but was caught and passed by Datson in a terrific ride, which broke Frogley's track record of 39.13 mph, setting a new speed of 39.30.

In the final, Datson took the lead from the start and never looked like being passed. Willimot fell on the second lap while Schlam came off at the start of the last lap. Meanwhile, Willimot had remounted and passed Schlam, just as the latter was also managing to remount. In a remarkable last lap,

Another of the pioneer Australians who rode at Crystal Palace, Sig Schlam.

Speedway's leading female rider in the early years of the sport, Fay Taylour. She rode at Crystal Palace several times in 1928.

Schlam kept his throttle wide open to catch Willimot and just pass him on the line, taking first place by half a length.

Britain's leading female rider, Fay Taylour, put in an appearance at Crystal Palace the following week and was having a tremendous tussle with Ron Johnson when she fell on the last lap. It was said that being a lady, her fall was 'most graceful', though for a moment she was standing on her head.

Arthur Willimot took the 1-mile scratch race final from Dick Bellamy, with Roger Frogley only managing third place on a borrowed machine. Datson made an attempt on his own track record but just missed out.

The season continued in a similar vein with the three Australians along with Frogley, Wills and Willimot tending to dominate the proceedings, though a number of the local path racers who had decided to try their hand at the new sport were beginning to make people sit up and take notice, with one in particular, Joe Francis, improving week by week.

In July, Johnnie Hoskins, who was still involved in the management of Crystal Palace by virtue of the fact that he was the manager of the three leading Australians, wrote an informative letter home.

Charlie Datson, Sig Schlam and Ron Johnson are doing well. They are still racing at the Crystal Palace, London. Charlie has a wonderful motor and last Saturday he put up what was described as a 'most lurid ride'. He holds the track record: in fact, I think it is the fastest time yet recorded on a small track here. He is quite an idol. Sig was in a scratch race last week and he was going so slowly round a corner that he fell off and his opponent passed him with one lap to go. Sig jumped on again and you know he goes when anyone is in front. He simply flew down the straight and just passed his man at the gun. The crowd of 20,000 went crazy. Ron has been having a lot of trouble with chains, but is riding wonderfully well. There were about 70,000 people at the Palace at a big sports gathering and Ron gave a wonderful exhibition of cinder throwing. The crowd gave him a great hearing … Charlie went out in an endeavour to break [his own track record] but missed by one second. Sig gave an exhibition of painting the fence with cinders and thrilled the crowd with the best show I have seen him put up yet. Some of the English riders have come along wonderfully well, and though they are not yet, in my opinion, up to the Australian, they are not far from it: in fact, we have to keep the motors in the very best condition to stand them off. On other tracks English riders have been beating Australians in some events.

Crystal Palace took part in its first-ever inter-track match on 25 July, racing away at Stamford Bridge. This took the form of three match races. Lionel

Wills won the first heat for Crystal Palace, beating Stamford Bridge's Bill Bragg, but in the second heat the result was reversed with Stamford Bridge's Dick Heller defeating Crystal Palace's Basil Greathurst. The deciding heat was won by Wills, who defeated Heller, thus claiming victory for Crystal Palace in their first-ever match.

The return took place on 28 July and this time Crystal Palace won 2-0, with Wills beating Bragg and Greathurst defeating Heller. Also on 28 July, the American, Art Pechar, was a guest at the track and broke the four-lap record in a special attempt with a speed of 41.5 mph.

The following week, on 4 August, Pechar returned to take on Roger Frogley in a match race. By the end of the third lap, Pechar was miles in front when his engine seized, allowing the Englishman through to win. The track record was broken yet again at this meeting when another visiting star, Australia's Paddy Dean, recorded 41.86 mph. The scratch race final that day saw Fay Taylour beat Roger Frogley's brother, Buster, into second place, while behind them, Bill Delaney, on his Rudge Special, crashed 100 yards from the finishing line. The report in *The Motor Cycle* of this incident makes amusing reading: 'Picking up his machine, he tried to Rudge it, not trudge it, but the bike not

The Frogley brothers – Buster, left, and Roger, right – who both rode at Crystal Palace in 1928. Roger Frogley was one of England's representatives in the first match at Crystal Palace and was probably the leading English rider in the early years of the sport in this country. He went on to ride for the Glaziers from 1929-32.

entering in to the spirit of the thing, he trudged to the line to the strains of slow music, gaining third place in four minutes two seconds.'

The meeting held on 18 August was generally acknowledged to be the best of the year, with every race being keenly contested. The main event of the day was a series of match races with a final between the four winners for the *News of the World* Belt. The four finalists were Roger Frogley, Arthur Willimot, Steve Pullen and Gordon Cobbold. Not surprisingly, Frogley won the final and the belt.

The next week, Lionel Wills challenged Frogley for the belt. Having been told the track was harder than usual, Wills spent 45 minutes before the race carefully fitting a new sprocket which would give him a higher gear ratio to the one he normally used. As it happened, the track was no harder than usual, leaving Wills unable to get out of the bends as fast as Frogley, allowing his opponent to retain his title.

The meeting on 1 September saw one of the great stars of the early years of speedway, the American Sprouts Elder, pay a visit to Crystal Palace to race a match race against Frogley. For three laps they were neck and neck, but Elder just got ahead on the last bend and filled Frogley in with flying cinders, taking the race by about four lengths.

Frogley's *News of the World* Belt challenge this week came from Joe Francis, who was now proving himself good enough to mix it with the best. They attempted to start the race no less than three times. In the first two, Francis fell on the first bend, and Frogley fell in the third. It was then announced that the challenge race would be abandoned, whereupon the crowd of some 23,000 rose to their feet protesting loudly and the decision was quickly reversed. Both riders got past the first bend at the fourth time of asking, with Frogley going on to retain his title.

By this time, Roger Frogley had established himself as one of the two best English riders in speedway, the other being Jim Kempster, a regular at Wimbledon. On 8 September, Kempster came to Crystal Palace to settle the question of who was the best English rider. Frogley got the better of his opponent, and much was said at the time about him being the unofficial English champion. Another inter-track match was held at this meeting with the Palace riders beating West Ham.

Crystal Palace had their first 'international' match on 15 September when they took on Edinburgh. Sadly for the home team, George MacKenzie and James Valenti beat Steve Pullen and Walter Harris respectively to give Edinburgh the victory. When Edinburgh returned for another match on 6 October, Crystal Palace ensured that they wouldn't lose again by putting out the Frogley brothers against George MacKenzie and Drew McQueen. This time Crystal Palace beat Edinburgh 2-0.

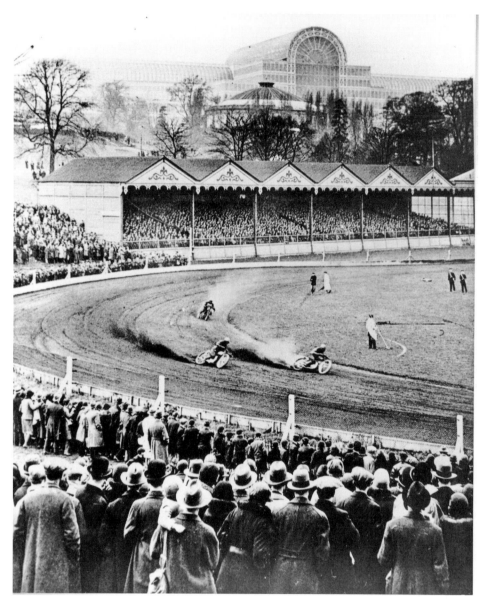

A view of the track with the Crystal Palace looming up in the background. Note the number of spectators.

The last meeting of the first season was held on 20 October. Another of the big stars of the pioneer days, 'Cyclone' Billy Lamont, was invited. Unfortunately it rained heavily before the meeting and about half an hour before it was due to start, water was pouring down the banking, washing all the cinders to the inside of the track. Lamont was known as 'the man with a month to live' because of his spectacular open throttle approach; wherever he went crowds flocked to see this round-the-boards thrill merchant. Sadly, because there was no dirt on the outside, Lamont was unable to ride his favourite line. Nevertheless his first match race with Frogley proved to be tremendous; the two riders were neck and neck for most of the race, with Frogley just getting through on the line. Race two saw a similar race, but this time it was Lamont who just won by half a length. The third race was going the same way until Lamont hit a large bump on the last lap sending him in to the fence and allowing Frogley to come home alone to win the series, 2-1. Frogley broke the track record in this race with a speed of 42.55 mph.

And so the season came to a fitting end, with Crystal Palace's undoubted star rider, Roger Frogley, beating one of the leading Australians. All meetings had been held during the afternoon, but it was announced at the final meeting that when Crystal Palace reopened on 30 March 1929, the meetings would be held at night as new electric flood lighting was to be installed over the winter.

1929

Although the 1929 season opened without the promised electric flood lighting, it did start with the visit of arguably the best rider in the world at that time, the Australian pioneer Frank Arthur. As expected, he defeated local hero Roger Frogley in a match race in a new track record time of 84 seconds (42.85 mph). But there was worse to come for Frogley as he also lost to former path rider, Triss Sharp, in one of the scratch race heats.

In the first match of the next meeting, Frogley pulled off a narrow victory against Billy Lamont in spite of a typically death defying last lap by the Cyclone, which saw him scraping the fence all the way round in his attempt to take Frogley on the outside. But the rest of the meeting was disastrous for Frogley who tried four different machines without any of them behaving itself.

Despite Crystal Palace's star attraction having a poor (for him) start to the season, the crowds still turned up in their thousands. By now speedway was becoming big business in this country and some of the riders – Vic Huxley,

Triss Sharp, no. 30, on his Calthorpe, taking part in the path racing.

Frank Arthur and Sprouts Elder, for example – were among the highest paid (if not *the* highest paid) sports stars in England. International Speedways Ltd. were the leading promoters in Australia and England with three London tracks – White City, Wimbledon and Harringay – to their name as well as more in the provinces; they were a very professional outfit running slick meetings. Although run by businessmen Mockford and Smith, there was more of a homely atmosphere at Crystal Palace. The promoters seemed to have the knack of treating the riders and officials as part of the family, with the result that they all wanted to give their best. This atmosphere filtered through to the crowds and the whole place was like a very big, happy family, and Crystal Palace became a popular destination, even for supporters of other tracks.

On 13 April, the first dead-heat at Crystal Palace occurred when Buster Frogley and Colin Ford crossed the line together after a thrilling race. Amazingly, this dead-heat was followed by another in the same meeting for third place of the first semi-final of the handicap event.

The track record topped 45 mph for the first time on 27 April when Ron Johnson broke both the flying four-lap record and the flying one-lap record, the former with a time of 43.93 mph and the latter with a time of 45.45 mph. Only two other tracks in the country, Stamford Bridge and Sheffield, could boast such a fast speed.

The third of the pioneer Australians who rode at Crystal Palace, Ron Johnson. Johnson was to remain with the Crystal Palace/New Cross setup until the final closure of the latter in 1963.

Over the 1928/29 close season, the speedway promoters had agreed to introduce league speedway into the country. During speedway's first season in Britain, all tracks had run meetings with a series of individual races, and maybe the odd 'inter-track' challenge between just two riders from each track. Some of the promoters had realised that the public would not go on forever accepting a meaningless succession of scratch races, and what they really wanted was to be able to cheer on their favourites in their own teams just as they did with football. Two leagues were formed, the English Dirt Track League for all the Northern tracks, and the Southern League for those in the south. Twelve teams, including Crystal Palace, entered the Southern League. However, other promoters were not so sure and felt that the public would not easily give up the idea of seeing the top men in the game pitted against each other every week. And so a compromise was reached. All riders were classed in to three groups, Star, A Grade and B Grade. The Star riders were banned from league teams and instead continued to ride against each other in the same way as before. Meeting programmes now consisted of six-heat league matches plus the individual races that had dominated the 1928 season.

With Star riders like Frogley and Johnson banned, the Crystal Palace team was made up of Triss Sharp, who, at the tender age of just 19, was appointed captain, Arthur Willimot, Joe Francis, Walter Harris, Bryan Donkin and Jack Barrett. They called themselves the Glaziers, though they also acquired the nickname in the press, 'The Glasshouse Boys'. Their first league fixture was away at White City on 3 May.

After two false starts, the first heat got underway as White City's Clem Cort shot into the lead past Willimott, with Harris close behind. When Willimott suffered engine failure it was up to Harris to do the chasing. He finally caught Cort on the last corner, coming through on the inside and up the final straight to become Crystal Palace's first-ever race winner. For that first season, four points were awarded for a win, two for second and one for third, so the Glaziers began with a 4-3 first heat. The second heat was another close race with Palace's Triss Sharp again taking his opponent, Dank Ewen, on the last bend, only this time doing it round the outside, resulting in

Triss Sharp (full name, Austin Charles Tristram Sharp), the Glaziers' first captain, rode for the team from 1929-33.

another 4-3. Incredibly, the third race went exactly the same way, with Joe Francis this time becoming the Glaziers' last bend hero as he took Freddy Hore on the inside. Three 4-3s, leaving Crystal Palace 12-9 up. The sequence of last bend overtakes came to an end in the next heat as Sharp led from start to finish, and with both Donkin and Cort falling, it was a 4-2 to the Glaziers. Crystal Palace suffered their only reverse of the match in the next race as Ewen came home in front of Francis and with Barrett falling; it was a 5-2 to White City. The Glaziers made up for that reverse in the last heat as Harris and Willimott took first and second place over their opponents to finish with a 6-1 victory, meaning that Crystal Palace won their first match 24-17, by a convincing margin of seven points. Point scorers were: Sharp 8, Francis 6, Harris 6, Willimott 4, Donkin 0, Barrett 0.

And so the scene was set for Crystal Palace's first home league fixture the following night, when the Glaziers took on South London neighbours, Wimbledon. Triss Sharp, captain and best rider, had suffered a slight injury in the second half the night before and was unavailable to ride. His place was taken by Crystal Palace's reserve, Fred Cooper. Consequently, when Bryan Donkin fell and injured himself during the match, Crystal Palace had no one to replace him with and they were forced to go into the last heat with only one rider. Fortunately by then it didn't matter as the rest of the team had ridden magnificently in front of their own supporters, with Harris scoring 8, Willimott 6, Francis 4 and Cooper in particular riding above himself to contribute five points. The final score was Crystal Palace 23 Wimbledon 19. The film star, Pauline Johnson, was a guest at the meeting and she congratulated the team on their victory.

In the second half, Frogley took on the Australian star, Max Grosskreutz, in a best of three match race series, beating him 2-0.

With the team away at Perry Barr the following Saturday, Ron Johnson dominated an individual meeting. He was in sensational form winning every event he raced in. Meanwhile, up in Birmingham, the Glaziers were not having things their own way, and for the first time they suffered a reverse, going down 26-16. Johnson himself had no problems with the Birmingham track, however, as the week after sweeping the board at Crystal Palace, he rode in eight races at Perry Barr and won all of those too, following this up with another seven out of seven at Birmingham two days later. Back at Crystal Palace five days later, he broke both the one-lap and the four-lap record.

As if the loss to Birmingham wasn't bad enough, Crystal Palace suffered their first home defeat in their next match, losing to Southampton 23-19. Sharp had returned and was in great form, scoring eight points and setting

The 1929 Crystal Palace Southern League Team. From left to right: George Lovick, Bryan Donkin, Arthur Willimot, Fred Mockford (manager, standing), Triss Sharp (captain), Joe Francis, Wally Harris, Jack Barnett.

One of speedway's first 'Superstars', the American, Sprouts Elder, roaring round the Crystal Palace track in 1928.

up the fastest time of the night, but apart from Harris, he received very little backing. Johnson meanwhile continued his superlative form in the second half, beating the American superstar Sprouts Elder 2-1.

After one more loss – 23-19 away to Wimbledon – the league format was changed. Several clubs, including Wimbledon and Harringay, complained that crowds were falling and that they would withdraw from the league as they felt that the customers still preferred the old style individual races. However, the national newspaper editors told a different story, that the crowds were dropping not because there was too much team racing, but because there wasn't enough of it. They said they would give the sport far more coverage if the main bulk of the meeting was handed over to the league competition and individual races were relegated to the secondary attraction. As a result, the promoters agreed to increase league matches to nine heats from the current six.

Crystal Palace's first match under the new system was away at Southampton. The team that had beaten them at home now beat them away as well. Only Donkin with 10 points, and Harris with eight, put up any form of resistance. The final score was 39-24 to the home team. Three days later, the Glaziers lost at home to West Ham. After four heats the scores were level, but the final five heats were all won by a West Ham rider, with the final score being Crystal Palace 28 West Ham 35. The only good thing about this match was the fact that Triss Sharp seemed to be getting back to his best form. He had had a couple of poor meetings against Wimbledon and Southampton, but this time he scored 9 points and was much more involved in the action. In fact, Sharp's form had been improved by his discovery of the best way to ride the Crystal Palace track. Letting the others go in front at the start he would swing across to the outside of the track on the first bend, then take a sharp left, cutting across the angle of the bend, inside the others to be first out of the second bend with his wheels in line.

These reverses were followed by two stunning victories over Wembley, 40-23 at the Empire Stadium and 42-21 back at Sydenham. Sharp's form continued to improve as he scored 10 at Wembley and then a maximum 12 at home. However, these two big victories were followed by two even bigger defeats as the Glaziers went down 46-17 at Coventry and 45-18 at Stamford Bridge.

Although the defeat at Stamford Bridge sounds bad, the Glaziers did manage to score more points than any other team had managed at the Bridge all season. In fact, Crystal Palace could well have scored more points as Joe Francis, who won two of his heats, shed a chain in heat one and Bryan Donkin did exactly the same in heat two. It was clear, even at this early stage, that Stamford Bridge would carry all before them and take the league title. Many complained that the nature of their track gave them an unfair home advantage as it was very narrow and quite unlike any of the others.

The boys from the Glasshouse bounced back from their defeat at Coventry by beating the same team 38-25 at home on 27 July, with Sharp once again scoring a maximum. Another loss, away at Harringay on 3 August by 37 points to 25 was followed by a run of five straight victories.

The first of these was a closely fought 32-31 win away at Lea Bridge with Sharp once again showing the way with a 12-point maximum. The return three days later was another exciting affair, although it started out looking like an easy victory for the Glaziers as they won four out of the first five heats, but a Lea Bridge rally in the second half of the match kept the score down to a respectable 34-29 victory for the home team. This time, Sharp's contribution of 10 points was ably supported by Donkin and Francis, both with eight. A special match race was held in the second half between the two leading female riders of the day, with Eva Askquith getting the better of Fay Taylour.

Before the next home match against Perry Barr on 24 August, Sharp fell and injured himself while attempting the flying one- and four-lap records; he was forbidden to ride in the rest of the meeting by the track doctor. Les Bowden was brought in as reserve but it looked as though the Glaziers could be in trouble without their high-scoring captain. However, the whole team rode above themselves, with both Jack Barrett and George Lovick scoring maximums and Donkin and Willimott adding a further eight each. Even without Sharp, Crystal Palace recorded their best win of the season with a 45-18 thumping of the opposition.

Sharp returned for the following week's match against Harringay and banged in yet another maximum, and with Donkin, Francis, Willimot and Barrett all winning one race each it was another easy win for the Glaziers, this time by 39 points to 23.

The next match, away at West Ham, opened with a sensational first heat as Sharp shot into the lead on the first bend. He managed to hold off the Hammers' captain, Tiger Stevenson, for four laps until the latter made a desperate move on the last bend and down the home straight, just catching Sharp on the line to take the verdict. West Ham followed up this win with another in the next heat, but in heat three Bryan Donkin led the Hammers all the way, and from there on, Crystal Palace slowly gained the ascendancy to run out winners at 38-25. Donkin scored his only maximum of the season, while Sharp added ten points.

Triss Sharp leads Lea Bridge's Jimmy Stevens and team mate, Joe Francis, in a scratch race event after the match on 10 August 1929.

The grand parade of riders before a meeting in 1929.

The first reverse in six matches came on 21 September when league champions Stamford Bridge visited the Palace. Sharp once again put in a maximum, but it wasn't enough to prevent the Pensioners taking the match 34-29. The last league match of the season for Crystal Palace resulted in another home win, this time over White City with a score line of 34-29.

In the end, the Glaziers finished a respectable fourth in the league with 22 points from twenty matches. As expected, Stamford Bridge had romped away with the league title with 34 points. Triss Sharp had been by far and away the most successful rider, racking up 142 points from sixteen matches, scoring seven maximums and four further double-figure scores. It is misleading to quote averages for this first season of the new league as results were not always recorded properly. For example, fourth place was never reported, so it is not always possible to confirm how many races each rider actually rode in. Also, in this first season, the riders only rode in two races for the first five matches and then three for the rest of the season and then, to add to the complication, four points were awarded for a win. Donkin put in a useful 97 from seventeen matches.

Triss Sharp rides round the outside of team mate, Joe Francis, on his way to victory in a scratch race held on 20 May 1929.

Meanwhile, while the league season was occupying the time of most of the Crystal Palace riders, their two stars, Roger Frogley and Ron Johnson, were taking part in the Star Riders' Championship. This was a new competition instituted by the *Star* newspaper and was run in two sections, Britain and Overseas, as it was felt that British riders were not yet equal to the Australians and Americans and would be overwhelmed. The Championship consisted of a series of match races between riders nominated by each of the Southern League teams (one for each section) apart from the two Birmingham teams. The match races were run on a home and away knockout basis, with each leg being decided over three races with the winners from the first round going through to a second round and then to a semi-final and final.

Johnson faced Wimbledon's Vic Huxley in the first round and came off second best as Huxley progressed. Unfortunately, this was not the end of Johnson's troubles for the year, as in a race at Exeter he scraped along the safety fence and felt a sharp pain in his right foot. When he looked down he saw his little toe hanging out of his boot. When he got to the hospital, the doctor asked him if he wanted to keep it and said they could stick it back on, plaster it and hope it would knit. He told Johnson it would probably take about three months to heal properly. Johnson was having none of that – he couldn't afford not to be earning for three months – so the doctor snipped the connecting skin and that was that.

For Frogley, however, things went a lot better. Having defeated Stamford Bridge's Gus Kuhn in the first round, and West Ham's Ivor Creek in the second, he found himself with a bye in the semi-final and therefore through to the final where he was due to meet Coventry's Jack Parker. Crystal Palace's last home meeting of the season was held on 12 October and saw Frogley defeat Parker in the first leg, but Parker had his revenge at Coventry and the final was decided at the neutral Wimbledon track on 21 October.

Unfortunately, a few days before the final, Frogley crashed in a race and was carried semi-conscious from the track. His injuries were so bad that he was bed-ridden until just a few hours before the final was due to take place. Getting out of bed, he realised that he was still very shaken and in no condition to race the race of his life. Frogley was a qualified pilot and so, to get himself going, he climbed into the cockpit of an aeroplane which was on the airfield at his father's farm in Hoddesdon, and went for a solo ride, carrying out as many stunt manoeuvres as he could remember. The shock treatment worked, and not only was he fit enough to ride, but he actually beat Parker to become the first British Star Riders' Champion and therefore prove himself as the best British rider in speedway.

1929 – Southern League

Date		Opponent		Score
3 May	A	White City	W	24-17
4 May	H	Wimbledon	W	23-19
11 May	A	Birmingham	L	16-26
1 June	H	Southampton	L	19-23
3 June	A	Wimbledon	L	19-23
26 June	A	Southampton	L	24-39
29 June	H	West Ham	L	28-35
4 July	A	Wembley	W	40-23
13 July	H	Wembley	W	42-21
18 July	A	Coventry	L	17-46
24 July	A	Stamford Bridge	L	18-45
27 July	H	Coventry	W	38-35
3 August	A	Harringay	L	25-37
7 August	A	Lea Bridge	W	32-31
10 August	H	Lea Bridge	W	34-29
24 August	H	Birmingham	W	45-18
31 August	H	Harringay	W	39-23
5 September	A	West Ham	W	38-25
21 September	H	Stamford Bridge	L	29-34
28 September	H	White City	W	34-29

Rider	M	Pts	Ave
Triss Sharp	16	142	8.88
Bryan Donkin	17	97	5.71
Wally Harris	7	38	5.43
Jack Barrett	11	51	4.64
George Lovick	14	60	4.29
Joe Francis	18	76	4.22
Arthur Willimott	18	74	4.11

Chapter Two

The Early 1930s

1930

The new season opened at Crystal Palace on 5 April. It had been agreed towards the end of the previous season that the star riders would now be allowed to ride in the league, so Mockford quickly signed up Frogley and Johnson and appointed Frogely captain. With Sharp remaining in the team, backed up by Donkin, Francis and Barrett, Crystal Palace looked very powerful and ready to take on the best in the League, which consisted of the same twelve teams plus King's Oak (High Beech) and Nottingham. It was announced that racing would commence at 7:00 p.m. during the months of May, June and July, but would continue at 3:30 p.m. for the rest of the season as the long-awaited floodlighting had still not been installed.

The two new stars of the team started the season in fine form as Johnson won the 'Big Six' event and Frogley the Handicap Final at the first meeting. Not to be left out of things, Sharp put up a brilliant performance at the Easter Monday meeting, breaking Frogley's standing start four-lap track record of 88.6 seconds with a time of 87.8, before going on to win the Handicap Final and beating Joe Francis for the *News of the World* Belt. Francis himself was having a good meeting, winning the 'Big Six' match race. This bank holiday meeting attracted an enormous crowd of 71,311 paying customers.

The Glaziers first match of the season was an away fixture at Harringay on 26 April. A large number of supporters travelled with the team to see Frogley defeat Harringay's two star men, Huxley and Colin Watson, and create a new track record. But, sadly for them, Johnson suffered engine failure in each of his three races and the team went down by 31 points to 22.

How the *News of the World* saw the 1929 Crystal Palace team.

With Johnson's engine behaving itself at the first home match against Stamford Bridge, the Glaziers recorded an impressive 34-19 victory over the league champions. Both Frogley and Johnson scored 9-point maximums (the race winner now scored three points instead of four) and Sharp added a further eight. Because meetings were starting at 7:00 p.m. and there was no floodlighting, the Palace management had to ensure that the meetings were staged efficiently and finished before it got dark. This one, match and second half, consisting of eighteen heats of racing, was all over in one and half hours, including an interval.

The Glaziers recorded an even bigger victory in their next match when they annihilated Perry Barr 36-18, winning every heat in the process. Shortly after this match, Perry Barr closed through lack of support and Mockford signed up their captain, Wally Lloyd, and Australian, Clem Mitchell, for the Crystal Palace team. Lloyd was put straight into the team ahead of Bryan Donkin who had had a poor start to the season, while Mitchell was made reserve. It was an indication of the strength of the Crystal Palace team that Mitchell could not get into the team proper, as in most other teams he would undoubtedly have been slotted straight in.

Another big victory over Harringay followed, this time by a score of 33 to 18, with Frogley making yet another maximum.

Although things were going well at home, the team were struggling a bit away, with the loss at Harringay being followed by further losses at Coventry, 20-34, and Wimbledon, 26-28. As befits a local derby, the match against Wimbledon was probably the most exciting match of the year, with the result in doubt until the last heat. Throughout the match there had never been more than two points in it. All but three heats resulted in 3-3 scores while Palace won one heat 4-2 and Wimbledon won two heats 4-2. A large number of Crystal Palace supporters had journeyed to the match in a long procession of cars and charabancs and certainly made their presence felt with their noise.

Another away loss at Wembley followed, causing the *Speedway News* to comment, 'Possibly the most disappointing team in the whole league is Crystal Palace with such riders as Frogley, Johnson and Sharp, one would

Bryan Donkin, who rode for the Glaziers in 1929-30.

think the Glaziers would be one of the hardest nuts to crack, but they have failed frequently when it comes to gathering league points. Roger Frogley, who makes a habit of winning all his league heats, again obliged for the Palace, and it must have been a very disappointed Roger who found that the others did not back up his victories.'

Although the Glaziers lost by a bigger margin, 22-31, this was also an exciting match with a number of races being decided on the line. For example, in heat one Sharp seemed to have the race well in hand until the last bend when he was overtaken by Arthur Atkinson who snatched victory by inches. Indeed most spectators thought the result would be given as a dead heat. One of Frogley's races too was not decided until the line. Catlett led at the first bend but was soon overtaken by Frogley and his new partner, Wally Lloyd. Just when it seemed like a certain 5-1 to Crystal Palace, Wembley's Harry Whitfield got between them and took the lead. Frogley chased after him overhauling him on the last lap to win by inches. Frogley's

Wally Lloyd, rode for Crystal Palace in 1930 and returned for the special August Bank Holiday meeting in 1939.

dominance was emphasised in the second half when he broke the one-lap record.

Perhaps stung by the criticism in the press, Crystal Palace overwhelmed league leaders Coventry in their next home match, winning 38-16 with the whole team playing their part in the victory. The Johnson/Francis combination was particularly lethal, gaining three 5-1s in their three outings together. Frogley and Sharp won two races each while Barrett and Lloyd both added five points. Only one Coventry rider managed to win a heat. That rider, significantly, was Tom Farndon, a name Crystal Palace was to hear much more of in the coming years.

The Glaziers' run of away defeats came to an end on 18 June when they took on and beat Southampton, who were second in the league. It was to some extent a surprising result, given the relative fortunes of the teams so far, but probably the main reason for Southampton's defeat was the number of engine failures the team suffered. However, this should not detract from Crystal Palace's performance as one of the things the team prided itself on was in keeping their machines in good working order so that they would not lose out in this manner. Frogley followed up his two away maximums at Wimbledon and Wembley with an 8-point haul. The reserve, Mitchell, was given two rides in place of Barrett and won them both, while Johnson also won two races.

Two more victories followed, the first 34-20 at home to Leicester. This time it was Sharp's turn to score a maximum nine. The second, away at Nottingham, when the Glaziers put up their best away performance of the season, running out victors by 37 points to 16. In every department the Crystal Palace riders were superior to their Nottingham counterparts. Their riding was better, and once again, their bikes were faster and more reliable thanks to the work of their mechanics. For the second time that season, the Johnson/Francis combination was unbeaten, and for the third time in four away matches, Frogley scored a maximum.

Crystal Palace were now unbeaten in four matches, but their fortunes came down to earth with a bump in the next meeting as they lost at home to their South London rivals, Wimbledon, 25-29. The defeat was caused by the three Wimbledon heat leaders – Jim Kempster, Billy Lamont and Dicky Case – riding at the top of their form. Although Sharp and Johnson both managed to get the better of Kempster, the other two went through the meeting undefeated, and in spite of his two defeats, Kempster did manage the seemingly impossible at Crystal Palace by beating Frogley. It was the last heat that finally turned the match in Wimbledon's favour. After heat eight the scores were Crystal Palace 23 Wimbledon 25. Case was first into the first bend but was quickly overtaken by Frogley who held his lead with Case nibbling at his back wheel the whole way until the last bend of the last lap when Case dashed round Frogley to win by inches. It had been a most thrilling finale to an excellent match fought in a friendly manner with much applause from the Palace crowd at the good riding of their opponents. With this victory, Wimbledon went to the top of the table.

Crystal Palace recovered their form in the next home match beating Hall Green 34-19. Apart from an engine failure from Francis while leading, the Johnson/Francis pairing were yet again undefeated, while Sharp added another maximum.

Unfortunately, Johnson suffered a serious hand injury in the second half of this match. He later described what happened:

> In the middle of a match race with Huxley, the breather on my crankcase worked loose. I put my left hand down to feel if the oil was coming out. Instead the primary chain whipped off the tops of two fingers. On talking the glove off there were the tops inside! The blood was pumping out, but grabbing my left wrist with the other hand I stopped the flow by pressure and walked across to the ambulance tent, which at the Palace, was situated in the middle of the grass centre. I was soon fixed up.

However, this accident put him out of action for six weeks, but even without him, Crystal Palace won their next two home matches against Wembley and Lea Bridge. Once again a big factor in Wembley's defeat was mechanical failure. In heat one, Jack Ormston was leading when his tyre burst; in heat two Harry Whitfield was also leading when his motor failed; and there was a double problem in heat four when Whitfield and Stan Catlett were holding a 5-1 over Sharp when they both suffered mechanical problems. Johnson's absence allowed Francis to become top scorer for the Glaziers for the first time in his own right.

Without Johnson, Crystal Palace needed the rest of the team to be firing on all cylinders. Unfortunately in the next away match at High Beech, Sharp was right off form, failing to score any points at all, leaving the Foresters to have things much their own way apart from two incident-packed heats. The first was heat five. Right from the start Frogley was involved in a terrific tussle with High Beech's Phil Bishop, with Bishop just holding the lead. Entering the third bend on the second lap, Bishop came down heavily. Frogley, thanks to brilliant evasive action, just missed the fallen rider, though he had to ride on to the centre green to do so. Harry Shepherd, who had returned to the Crystal Palace team in place of Barrett, was not so fortunate and crashed into

Bishop while High Beech's other rider, Phil's brother, George, laid down his bike to avoid the others. While all this was going on, Frogley continued to race and completed another lap but was then shown the red flag for leaving the track. After some deliberation, however, the ACU Steward awarded him the race, making the score for the heat 3-0.

Frogley and Shepherd were both involved in the second eventful heat of the afternoon, heat seven. In this one, Frogley's motor packed up on the first lap, at the same time as Syd Edmonds' bike slowed up. Then at the end of the second lap, while well in the lead, the Foresters' captain, Jack Barnett, also slowed leaving Shepherd to catch and pass him to take the three points. In spite of these two gifted wins, Crystal Palace still lost the match by 21 points to 29.

In the evening, Sharp rode in the second half at Lea Bridge. In a match race against Jimmy Stevens, the latter's bike seized and Sharp crashed in to him, breaking his leg.

In spite of the loss of two of their heat leaders, Crystal Palace still managed to win their next home match against Lea Bridge, but only just as the final score was 27-26. The man mainly responsible for the Glaziers' victory was Jack Barrett, who had been dropped just a couple of weeks earlier. The scores going into the last heat were Crystal Palace 25 Lea Bridge 22, leaving Lea Bridge needing a 5-1 for victory. With Charlie Spinks and Alf Foulds shooting off into the lead it looked all over for the Glaziers, but suddenly, seemingly from nowhere, Barrett came through the centre of the pair, passing Foulds and salvaging the vital point that gave victory to the home side. Just as he crossed the line, Barrett's motor seized. In all Barrett scored seven points.

Shortly after this, it was announced that the *Evening News* would be sponsoring a new cup, the London Cup, to be raced for by the eight clubs in and around the London area. It was to be run on an eight-a-side sixteen-heat format.

Crystal Palace were drawn against local rivals, Wimbledon, in the first round. The first leg was held at Crystal Palace on 16 August. Ron Johnson returned for this match and showed he had lost none of his form by scoring 11 points. This together with Frogley's maximum 12 gave the Glaziers a first leg lead of 9 points at 52-43, and high hopes of knocking Wimbledon out of the London Cup.

Before the second leg was held, Crystal Palace took on Nottingham, and even without Sharp they almost managed a complete whitewash of the hapless Outlaws, winning 41-12. Only an engine failure from Frogley while leading prevented the final score from being 43-10. A Crystal Palace rider won every heat while the Johnson/Francis partnership was once again undefeated.

With this morale booster under their belt, the Glaziers travelled to Plough Lane with high hopes of progressing through to the next round of the London Cup, but within just five heats their 9-point lead had been pulled back by Wimbledon. Once again Lamont rode brilliantly and was ably supported by their American star, Ray Tauser. Both of them scored a maximum. Crystal Palace did not win a heat until the eighth, when Frogley defeated Case after a splendid race with plenty of passing and repassing. Johnson then beat the Wimbledon captain, Jim Kempster, but it was all too late and the Glaziers went down 62-33, losing the tie on aggregate, 85-105.

The next home match was against Southampton. Crystal Palace were the only team to beat Southampton at Bannister Court so it was reasonable to assume that they would beat them on their own track, but things didn't turn out that way and the Glaziers suffered their third home defeat of the season. The match started well for Crystal Palace when Frogley beat Sprouts Elder, but the second heat brought the first visit to Sydenham of Arnie Hansen. If most people thought that Billy Lamont was spectacular, this man was something else. Right from the start, the little Australian flew round the outside of the track at an incredible speed, looking as though he was about to career into the fence at every turn, but somehow he managed to stay on the bike and by the end of the second lap, Johnson was left trailing far behind. As he entered the first bend on the third lap he once again almost slid into the fence and just about managed to right himself in time. At this point he eased up slightly but still won the race by a large margin. After his first heat defeat, Elder won his remaining two races. In heat six he got away in front of Clem Mitchell and at every corner showered him with cinders. Mitchell's bike got so filled in that it packed up. Although there was nothing wrong with Elder's tactics it could be said that it was literally dirty riding! By the end of heat eight Southampton held a 6-point lead so that going into the last heat they were unassailable; with nothing riding on it the spectators were not expecting much to happen. But they were reckoning without Arnie Hansen again. The two Crystal Palace riders took the lead from the start and held it for the first two laps. Hansen was trailed off in last place. Suddenly he came to life and shot round the outside on bends one and two of the third lap, passing all three in one breathtaking overtake. He held on to win the heat and give Southampton a 30-24 victory.

Crystal Palace's last home match resulted in a 29-24 victory over High Beech with Johnson scoring a maximum.

Away from home, the Glaziers were not faring so well and between 15 July and 20 September they lost four out of four matches, including one heavy

Another view of the Crystal Palace track.

defeat at Stamford Bridge where they went down 19-35, with only Frogley and Johnson putting up any real resistance.

The Glaziers last match of the year was away at Lea Bridge on 1 October. With just two heats to go, they led by one point, 21-20, with their two best riders, Frogley and Johnson, still to come. As he came out on to the track for heat eight, Frogley's exhaust pipe looked very insecure, and sure enough just as the race started it came adrift. Although he managed to lead in to the first bend, Charlie Spinks and Stu Fairbairn caught and passed him, one on each side. Fairbairn shut him out at the next corner and Frogley was unable to get back into the race. Lea Bridge were now 3 points in front with one heat to go. Johnson took the lead from the start but Lovick was a poor fourth and when Johnson fell on the third lap it was a second successive 5-1 defeat to Lea Bridge, giving them the match at 30-23.

Not surprisingly, Frogley finished the season as Crystal Palace's top scorer with 150 points at an average of 6.82 (out of nine). Although hampered by injuries, both Sharp and Johnson also averaged over 6 with Triss scoring 105 points at an average of 6.18 and Johnson 110 points at an average of 6.11. Following a good end of season run when he finally managed to break into the team, Beckett was next with an average of 4.00 from ten matches.

On an individual level it had been a year of mixed fortunes for the three Crystal Palace heat leaders.

The formula for finding the Star Riders' champion was changed. There were no longer two sections, and the qualification for the final was now to be the top twelve scorers in the league as at the end of August. This was unfortunate for Johnson as he had missed part of the season through injury and did not gain enough points to qualify. Frogley qualified in third place with 104, the same as Harringay's Vic Huxley, behind Stamford Bridge's Frank Arthur on 113.5 and Wembley's Jack Ormston on 106. Triss Sharp also qualified in sixth place on 97 points, but by the time the final was held he was out injured and unable to take part. In the final, Frogley was drawn in heat two against Leicester's Syd Jackson and Hall Green's Harry Taft, but fell and lost his chance of retaining his title.

Another big individual event was held for the first time, the London Riders' Championship. With the final being held at Crystal Palace, Frogley and Johnson were very much among the favourites to take the title. There were twenty-seven riders in the final. The first round was a series of nine elimination heats in which three riders took part with the first two going through to the first round proper, which consisted of six heats of three riders. From there six went through to two semi-finals to race in two heats of three. The final was a match race between the two winning semi-finalists.

In the elimination round, Frogley won the first heat from Jack Ormston, equalling the track record as he did so. Lamont had been level with Frogley for three laps, but coming out of the second bend of the third lap he hit the fence and fell. Ormston was well behind at the time and never looked in with the remotest chance of qualifying for the first round until Lamont's mistake. Johnson won his heat but Francis came third in his while Lloyd fell.

In the first round proper, Frogley qualified for the semi finals by winning heat one from Ray Tauser while Johnson suffered engine failure in his race, putting him out.

Frogley was drawn in what looked like the weaker of the two semi-finals against Ormston and Wal Phillips, but he fell leaving Ormston to go through to the final. Bluey Wilkinson qualified from the other semi-final after Huxley hit several bumps which wrenched his rear tyre off.

The final was won by Jack Ormston. Although, in the end he proved to be a worthy winner, there is no doubt that he would never have got through the

The 1930 Crystal Palace Southern League team. From left to right: Triss Sharp, Ron Johnson, Harry 'Shep' Shepherd, Clem Mitchell, Wally Lloyd, Joe Francis, Roger Frogley (captain), Fred Mockford (manager).

elimination round if Lamont hadn't hit the fence on lap three of the very first race of the night.

One final honour went to Frogley and Johnson when they were chosen to represent their respective countries in the first-ever official Test match to be held. This took place on 30 June at Wimbledon. Australia had by far the better of the encounter, winning as they did 35-17. Frogley was the pick of the English riders, top scoring for the home side with 6 points, including one of the only two race wins by an Englishman. Johnson partnered Frank Arthur to two 5-1s out of the three races they rode in together, finishing the evening with five points.

The Crystal Palace management were lucky that they had some magnificent facilities on hand to keep their supporters together over the winter. They were able to put on big shows and dances in the central transept of the Palace itself, which were staged every week and proved to be immensely popular. The shows were supplemented by whist drives between the acts for those not wishing to dance. The cost for an evening's entertainment was 2/- (10p) per head for members of the general public and 1/6 (7½p) for supporters wearing their club badge.

Over the close season it was announced that Roger Frogley, together with his brother, Buster, were forming an aeroplane club on their father's farm at Hoddesdon, using about 50 acres.

1930 – Southern League

26 April	A	Harringay	L	22-31
1 May	A	Coventry	L	20-34
3 May	H	Stamford Bridge	W	34-19
17 May	H	Harringay	W	33-18
22 May	A	Leicester	D	27-27
26 May	A	Wimbledon	L	26-28
31 May	H	West Ham	L	22-32
12 June	A	Wembley	L	22-31
14 June	H	Coventry	W	38-15
18 June	A	Southampton	W	29-25
21 June	H	Leicester	W	34-20
26 June	A	Nottingham	W	37-16
28 June	H	Wimbledon	L	25-29
12 July	H	Hall Green	W	34-19
15 July	A	West Ham	L	23-31
19 July	H	Wembley	W	30-23
26 July	A	High Beech	L	22-29
9 August	H	Lea Bridge	W	27-26
15 August	A	Hall Green	L	26-28
23 August	H	Nottingham	W	41-12
6 September	H	Southampton	L	24-30
20 September	H	High Beech	W	29-24
20 September	A	Stamford Bridge	L	19-35
1 October	A	Lea Bridge	L	23-30

London Cup

First round

16 August	A	Wimbledon	L	33-62
8 September	H	Wimbledon	W	52-43

Lost 85-105 on aggregate

Rider	M	Pts	Ave
Roger Frogley	22	150	6.82
Triss Sharp	17	105	6.18
Ron Johnson	18	110	6.11

Clem Mitchell	10	40	4.00
Joe Francis	22	86	3.91
Wally Lloyd	13	49	3.77
Jack Barrett	14	41	2.93
Harry Shepherd	8	17	2.13

1931

The 1931 season started with great optimism. Now that his broken leg had completely healed, Triss Sharp was ready to return, joining Frogley and Johnson to form one of the best heat-leader trios in the league. Clem Mitchell, Joe Francis, George Lovick and Harry Shepherd were also still available while a place had to be found for newcomer, the young up and coming star, Tom Farndon, who had agreed to join Crystal Palace after the demise of Coventry at the end of the previous season.

Mockford hoped that with the experience gained the previous season, his team would be able to perform better on the away tracks. He had no doubts that they could beat every other team at Sydenham, but it was getting points away from home that had been the team's problem.

The 1931 Crystal Palace Southern League team. From left to right: Tom Farndon, Alf Sawford, Bill 'Skid' Pitcher, Joe Francis, Harry 'Shep' Shepherd, Fred Mockford (manager), Triss Sharp, Roger Frogley (captain), Nobby Key, Ron Johnson.

The season opened with a successful attempt on the one-lap track record by Wembley's Colin Watson, who got round in 19 seconds at a speed of 48.33 mph. Not only was this a track record for Crystal Palace, but it also beat Wal Phillips' fastest lap at Stamford Bridge, making it the fastest quarter of a mile ever recorded anywhere in the country. Later on in the second half, Watson won the scratch race final at a speed of 45.91 mph, setting up a new four-lap record.

The team's season started with an exciting home and away tie with Wimbledon for the South London Championship, with a 30-22 victory at home and a 23-31 loss away, making the final aggregate score 53-53.

The following week, the league campaign got underway with a victory over Lea Bridge. Although it was a convincing victory by 31 points to 21, it has to be said that this was more due to the moderate form showed by the opposition rather than great riding from the Glaziers. Frogley was absent for the match and Sharp was not yet back to his best form. The two best riders for Crystal Palace were Johnson and Francis, who rode as a pair and scored three perfect 5-1s, although originally Johnson was disqualified in the last heat for looking round while leading, but he was later reinstated on appeal. Shepherd's pre-season form had been poor, leading sceptics to ask how he came to distinguish himself so much in South Africa over the winter. However, he came good in this match, winning two heats and suffering engine failure while leading in his third.

Everyone was looking to see how Farndon would fit into the team. He made a reasonable debut but was also plagued by mechanical problems. He was, for example, winning the fifth heat and coming out of the fourth bend on the last lap, when his back wheel suddenly parted company with the rest of his bike. Fortunately he was able to pick himself up and stagger over the line with what was left of his motor, gaining second place as the two Lea Bridge riders had previously crashed into each other. In fact, one of them, Howie Osment, finished before Farndon but had not commenced his last lap when Shepherd, the winner, crossed the line, so he was disqualified.

The next match was away at West Ham, where, in spite of Frogley's return from New Zealand where he had been a member of the first English side to tour that country, the Glaziers were literally hammered, 33-19, with only Johnson putting up any sort of show.

The next visitors to Sydenham were Southampton, a team hitherto unbeaten at Crystal Palace and one of those most strongly fancied to take the league title. But they put up a poor performance with only Jack Parker able to match the home side. With Frogley back on form and Johnson and Francis once again proving to be a formidable pairing, the home side

Tom Farndon with his bike after the back wheel had come off in the match against Lea Bridge on 11 April 1931.

ran out victors, 30-24. Farndon once again suffered from multiple engine failures. The *Speedway News* reported that the match was 'dismally uninteresting'.

A good victory over Wimbledon at 32-22, in which Farndon scored his first victory in Crystal Palace colours, defeating Wimbledon star, Dick Case, was followed by a close run win, 26-24, over another strongly fancied side, Stamford Bridge. Once again the Johnson/Francis pairing proved decisive, taking 12 points out of a possible 15 between them. Stamford Bridge were unlucky that Arthur Warwick had such a poor afternoon, only managing to score one point for them, though he was very unfortunate in heat five when his engine seized just a yard or two from the line, losing him second place. Farndon once again had engine problems but rode well in the one heat he was free of them. Palace supporters were beginning to get impatient at his failure to sort his motors out, especially when they could see how well he could go when he was able to.

The second half saw the guest appearance of northern star, Joe Abbott, the first time a rider from the English Dirt Track League had ridden in the south that year. He was to have been accompanied by Ginger Lees, but

Joe Francis, who rode for the
Glaziers from 1929 to 1933.

unfortunately Lees had been injured and was unable to appear. Abbott took
a while to get used to the track, but in his third ride, although starting off
slowly, he was able to overtake and beat Francis.

The following meeting – away at Harringay – started disastrously for the
Glaziers. In the first heat both riders –Frogley and Shepherd – fell, and were
unable to remount, and in the second, machine problems prevented Johnson
from turning out at all, his place being taken by George Lovick who fell
just before completing two laps. The final score was Harringay 30 Crystal
Palace 21.

This defeat was nothing compared to the drubbing the Glaziers then
received at the hands of the Wembley Lions in their next match. At no time
did Crystal Palace look like putting up any sort of fight and the final score of
Wembley 41 Crystal Palace 12 was a fair reflection of the meeting. Not one
of the Crystal Palace team won a race, nor did they even manage to achieve

a single 3-3. Only two incidents stood out in the match: the first was in heat eight when the starter absent-mindedly held out the chequered flag as the riders approached the end of the third lap before he suddenly realised his mistake and dashed back to his neatly arranged flag-stand to get the right flag; and the second was the following heat which had to be restarted no less than seven times before the steward considered it to be a fair start. Wembley's Jack Ormston was fined for his part in this fiasco.

The optimism at the beginning of the season was now beginning to fade rapidly, and although the Glaziers managed to scrape through with a single-point victory in the next match – 27-26 at home to Harringay – it was far from a convincing victory. In fact, Harringay held a 1-point lead going in to the final heat. Harringay's Alf Sawford shot out into the lead at the start, but Triss Sharp was able to get past him. Behind them there was a terrific duel going on for the all-important third place point between Francis and Harringay's Durant, with Francis just coming out on top, giving the home side a narrow 4-2 win. The dominant rider in the meeting had been Harringay's great Australian star, Vic Huxley, who scored a maximum. The brightest spot for Crystal Palace was the return to form of Sharp, who suffered only one loss all afternoon at the hands of Huxley. It was the same old story yet again for Farndon. He scored six points, but in one heat he was leading when his chain broke and he had to wheel home for a single point.

Another close match followed and another victory as the Glaziers won away at Lea Bridge, 25-23, thanks to a last heat 4-2 from Johnson and Farndon. Unfortunately, just as he seemed to be coming back to something like his old form, Sharp began to be troubled again by the leg he had broken the season before, and after two pointless rides, he withdrew from his last one.

In spite of a good start in the next match away at High Beech, the Glaziers suffered defeat. Three points up after five heats, the match gradually slipped away from them and High Beech led by 1 point going into the last race. However, with Johnson and Farndon out for Crystal Palace, there was every hope that they could turn the match round. After two laps, Johnson led with Farndon in third place, meaning that the Glaziers held a 4-2 and a match winning score. However, coming into the second corner of the third lap, Johnson went slightly out of control and High Beech's Bobbie Blake cut through on the inside. Coming into the straight, Blake drifted wide and Johnson touched his rear wheel, wrenching out some spokes from his own front wheel and causing him to fall. Farndon, following close behind, could not avoid Johnson's machine and he fell as they collided. Meanwhile Blake had also lost control and fell, leaving Reg Hutchings, the sole surviving rider, to come in for a 3-0 for High Beech and a 27-23 defeat for Crystal Palace.

The run of last heat deciders came to an abrupt end two days later, on 27 May, as Crystal Palace lost away at Stamford Bridge. In spite of losing, the Glaziers made a real fight of it, Francis in particular, who managed to beat home-track favourites Wal Phillips and Arthur Warwick before losing out to Gus Kuhn in his third race after leading him by some distance before suffering mechanical problems.

It was a return to the last heat decider in the next match at home against West Ham, as going into the last heat the scores were level. This saw Francis and Sharp out against the Hammers' strongest pairing of Bluey Wilkinson and Reg Bounds, who proved just too strong for the home pair, taking a 4-2 and the match 27-25.

Home and away matches against Nottingham followed, both ending in victory for the respective home sides by similar margins as Nottingham beat Crystal Palace 29-25 at the Olympic Speedway, and the Glaziers returned the compliment, defeating the Outlaws 29-24 back in Sydenham.

A new competition was introduced in 1931 called the National Trophy. This was the first time that teams from the North and South had met in official competition. Sadly, Crystal Palace suffered a heavy defeat in their first National Trophy match, a second-round first-leg tie against Wimbledon, going down 60-36, only Johnson putting up much of a fight, while in the second leg they could only manage a 48-48 draw. They were out of the National Trophy before they could meet any of the northern teams.

There was a small diversion from speedway on 14 June as the official opening of the Broxbourne Aerodrome in Hertfordshire took place. Freddie Mockford was chairman of the directors, while two of his fellow directors and founders of the club were the Frogley brothers. An air pageant was organised in which the Frogleys took a prominent part, along with other speedway riders, Jim Kempster and Arthur Franklyn.

Back on the track the following week, Crystal Palace suffered their heaviest league defeat of the season going down 36-16 to a rampant Wembley Lions team. The only crumb of comfort came in the second half as the Crystal Palace reserves beat the Wembley Cubs 14-11 with Nobby Key scoring a maximum six points.

Two more crushing defeats followed, 36-18 at Southampton, and even worse, 40-13 at Wimbledon. The Glaziers tumbled to seventh place in the league and it was obvious that something radical had to be done to reverse this alarming decline in Crystal Palace's fortunes.

The first innovation was to put on special meetings every Thursday evening aimed at unearthing some junior talent. These were not training sessions as such but enabled young riders to race against each other gaining valuable experience under the watchful eye of Freddie Mockford who hoped to find riders of the future. This, of course, was more of a long-term solution and Mockford was still keen to come up with some short-term answers.

In the meantime, Crystal Palace lost yet another match, this time away at Coventry, but at least this time they put up a much better show in what was a thriller of a meeting with the lead changing hands practically every race. Going in to the final heat the score was 26-22 to Coventry, with Crystal Palace needing a 5-1 to level the match. With Farndon riding on his old track and Johnson out for the Glaziers, the visiting fans had every hope that they could succeed. Farndon had so far proved to be the best of the visitors, winning his first two races easily. The two immediately went off into the lead, but as had happened so often before, Farndon's machine let him down and he had to pull out, leaving Johnson to come in on his own for a 3-3, leaving

Tom Farndon, a leading candidate for the title 'greatest speedway rider of all time' rode for Crystal Palace from 1931 to 1933. Here he shows the spectacular riding action that made him such a firm favourite with the Crystal Palace fans.

Crystal Palace four points down at 29-25. This match was Nobby Key's senior team debut for the Glaziers, and although he only scored two points, it was obvious that he was going to prove a valuable asset for the team.

Away at High Beech for their next match on 4 July, it looked to start with as though Crystal Palace were on the way back. With two 5-1s in the first two heats, the Glaziers were 8 points up after just two heats. But after that it all went horribly wrong for them as High Beech won the next seven races as they pleased. Heat seven was the worst for Crystal Palace as Francis fell and Farndon piled into him. Although both escaped serious injury, the resulting 5-0 for the Forresters summed up the way the match was going. The final score was High Beech 32 Crystal Palace 20.

But there was quick revenge for the Glaziers; just 3½ hours later there was a complete turn-around back at Sydenham. Although Farndon was given a rest at reserve and did not actually ride due to his tumble earlier in the day, the final score was 32-20, Crystal Palace the victors with Francis, mounted on his new Wallis J.A.P., scoring a 9-point maximum. He was in such good form that in the second half he knocked a massive 1.2 seconds off the standing start record.

There was another last heat decider in their next match at Belle Vue who had come into the league following the demise of Harringay after fourteen matches. Although Belle Vue already had a team in the Northern League, they agreed to enter another team in the Southern League to take over Harringay's fixtures. To avoid confusion, Belle Vue's Southern League team was called Manchester. The final score was Manchester 28 Crystal Palace 26. Farndon was back with 8 points and Key added a useful 5, including a victory in the last heat, in which his partner, Johnson, lost out to Clem Cort for second place.

Following the earlier announcement that Crystal Palace were to run special meetings on Thursdays for junior riders, they were inundated with applications from all over southern England. Mockford announced that the meetings would last between one and one and a half hours with a total of twelve events. Prize money would be paid, and any rider who managed to win all his races would walk off with £15. The only condition laid down before a junior could enter was that he had to complete six laps of the track without falling off within a certain time-limit.

An easy home win against Coventry, 32-20, followed before the match that every club considered the 'big one' as it was the ambition of every team to beat Wembley. Wembley had been far and away the most successful team since the beginning of league speedway in 1929. Mockford realised that one of the main reasons for this was the care and attention the Wembley management paid to the team's bikes and he was determined to outdo Wembley in this department in his ongoing effort to take Crystal Palace to the top. Therefore, before the Wembley match, he made sure that all the team's machines were stripped down and cleaned, older parts replaced, and the engines tuned to perfection. The result was a stunning 30-23 victory over the champions, and not only that, but for the first time that season, it was clear that the Wembley bikes were not as fast as those of their opponents. The Farndon/Francis pairing scored a maximum 15 points, while Johnson scored an individual maximum.

Mockford now knew for sure that this was the way to go and so he set up a 'state-of-the-art' workshop at the back of the speedway track in the old polo pony sheds, fitted with all the best modern appliances for all the team members to use. Not only that, but Mockford brought in G. L. Wallis as workshop supervisor, the man whose bike frame, along with the J.A.P. engine, had revolutionised the sport. Along with four assistant mechanics, Mockford made Wallis responsible for ensuring that the Glaziers turned out in every match with the best possible machinery. Johnson, Francis, Key and Shepherd were all given brand new Wallis J.A.P. mounts, with another being made for Frogley. After every meeting, Wallis insisted on taking the bikes into the workshop and overhauling them. The only slight fly in the Mockford ointment was Tom Farndon, who insisted on continuing to look after his own machine. This wouldn't have been quite so bad if Farndon had been an expert mechanic himself, but he wasn't, and it was said that Mockford had to employ a special member of staff whose job it was to walk round the track and pick up the bits and pieces that had fallen off Farndon's bike during the racing.

The next home match against Southampton underlined the wisdom of Mockford's decision as the Glaziers hammered the Saints 38-15. There was no doubting the fact that their bikes were several miles an hour faster than the Southampton mounts. Johnson recorded the fastest race time ever seen at Crystal Palace when he stormed home in heat three in a time of 79.6 seconds. There now seemed every prospect of a much better second half to the season, although by now the league title was out of their reach, being in fifth place with 20 points from twenty-three matches, while Wembley were top with 32 from just nineteen matches.

The next home meeting was the Crystal Palace round of the Star Riders' Championship. A change in how to qualify for the final had been announced at the beginning of the season. This year, each club was to hold an elimination contest on its own track to find one of its representatives, while the second would be nominated by the club. Crystal Palace's contest was expected to be a close run thing between Johnson, Farndon and Francis, but it was Harry Shepherd who won the qualifier and so became the unexpected first representative for the Glaziers at the final. Farndon suffered engine failure in the first heat, while in the final, which was between Shepherd, Johnson, Francis and Triss Sharp, Johnson ran into Francis as the two were battling it out for the lead, leaving Shepherd to come in first in front of Sharp.

The only two teams in with any chance at all of overhauling Wembley for the league title were Stamford Bridge and West Ham, and it was Stamford Bridge who were next to oppose the Glaziers. But once again, it was the Wallis J.A.P.s that ruled the day as Crystal Palace more or less put paid to the Pensioners' chances of league success with a 31-23 victory. A 36-18 win over Coventry followed, with this time the Johnson/Key pairing taking a 15-point maximum haul.

A good away victory at Lea Bridge came next, as the Glaziers romped home with a score of 32-22.

Since the inauguration of the Southern League in 1929, races had been started by the rolling start method with the four riders coming up to the line together at approximately 15 mph as the flag fell. However, there were many false starts as riders tried to gain a slight advantage. Crystal Palace seemed to suffer more than most from this and held the record for twenty-six false starts in one meeting. Towards the end of August, new rules were brought in to try and combat this by drawing a line 4 yards behind the starting line, with the speed of the riders being determined by the rider on the inside. A race could only be started if at least the first three the riders had both wheels between the two lines. The new system worked better for a while, but it was something that speedway in general and the Crystal Palace management in particular would return to.

The second London Riders' Championship was held on 22 August and was a triumph for the home riders as the final was between Joe Francis and Ron Johnson, with the former winning by six lengths.

With Harry Shepherd already qualifying as the Crystal Palace representative in the Star Riders' final, the club held a vote among its supporters to decide on the second representative. This turned out to be Johnson. Sharp was the nominated reserve.

The two legs of the *Evening News* London Cup semi-finals were the next two meetings for the Glaziers. With their new found confidence resulting from their immaculate machinery, the supporters were convinced that their team would at last pick up their first trophy. And, indeed, Crystal Palace did pretty much as they pleased against Lea Bridge, winning the first leg away,

55-41 and the second by the massive score of 69-27. Johnson, Farndon and Francis were all practically unbeatable in both legs.

With Wembley beating Stamford Bridge in the other semi-final, the stage was set for the final the whole speedway world wanted to see. The old established champions against the new form team.

But before the final could take place there were some more league fixtures to get through, the next being against West Ham, currently placed second in the league. But once again, the Glaziers overwhelmed their opposition, winning 32-22. This was followed by an away victory at Southampton, 32-21.

Although the team was now at the top of its form, individual success was eluding them and when the Star Riders' final was held on 17 September, neither Shepherd nor Johnson got any further than the first round. Wimbledon's American star, Ray Tauser, proved to be the winner.

The Glaziers' final league match before the London Cup final was away at Coventry. This resulted in a confidence-boosting dismantling of the Bees, as Crystal Palace ran out winners 35-19. Once again it was noted that the difference in the speed of the bikes was a notable factor in the victory.

And so to the first leg of the London Cup final. Not for the first time, Johnson, Farndon and Francis were all but unbeatable. Johnson scored a maximum 12 points; Farndon scored 9 from three races and then fell in his last heat, while Francis also won three heats out of three, having been disqualified in heat fourteen for twice jumping the start. And with the support of Sharp, 6 paid 9 from three races plus one engine failure, the first leg resulted in a stunning victory for the form team, as Crystal Palace recorded a 59-36 win.

Everything now seemed set for an exciting return leg at Wembley. There was a feeling among neutrals and supporters of both teams that the second leg would consist of a long and keen struggle by the Lions to make up the 23-point deficit, and that the interest would come in seeing if the Glaziers could hang on enough to take the title.

But that wasn't how it turned out. Hundreds of Crystal Palace fans made the trip to Wembley to cheer on their team, forming a colourful orange and black section among the 35,000 crowd. It came as a joyous surprise to them, and as something of a shock to the Wembley supporters, when Farndon took charge in the very first heat, overwhelming the Wembley captain, Colin Watson, to take the first heat in the very fast time of 79 seconds. But it was not only that which excited the Glaziers' fans; behind him, Frogley overtook Watson on the last corner to give Crystal Palace a 5-1 and increase the lead to 30 points. Wembley pulled back two points in the next heat, but from then on they did not win another heat until well in to the second half, after the Glaziers had been assured of victory.

Such was the mastery of the Glaziers' performance that after just nine of the sixteen heats, it came to the point where Wembley needed a 5-0 in every remaining heat just to draw. Once again, it was the trio of Johnson, 12 points, Farndon, 12, and Francis, 11, who put paid to the Lions' chances. The final score was Wembley 40 Crystal Palace 55, making the aggregate score Crystal Palace 114 Wembley 76. It was a comprehensive thrashing of supposedly the best team English speedway had ever seen.

It was Crystal Palace's first trophy and Wembley's first home defeat in a cup tie.

This was exciting enough, but there was more to come. The very next home meeting was a league match against Manchester. Before the match started the London Cup was presented to the team by the assistant editor of the *Evening News*, Mr A. E. Olly, and the team paraded round the track on the back of a lorry in front of their deliriously happy fans. In a nice touch, and in recognition of the important part he had played in bringing the London Cup back to Sydenham, A. G. Wallis was asked to take part in the parade with the riders.

Having got the formalities over, the Glaziers set about Manchester, and in one of the most amazing matches of all time, they completely whitewashed them 45-9, winning every single heat 5-1. This had never been done before, and has only been done on a handful of occasions in the eighty-one years since. Ironically, before that the record lowest score had been recorded by Crystal Palace themselves, when they had lost to Wembley managing just 11 points. The *Speedway News*, which usually gave a report of each race in a match, gave one report which covered every race: 'At the fall of the flag the pair wearing orange and black would dash ahead of the Manchester lads, lead them through the first corner, and win at leisure.'

There was absolutely no doubt at all that the Crystal Palace team were now the best in the country. From their point of view it was a shame the improvement had come too late to give them a chance of the league title. The performances of Crystal Palace gave rise to an editorial in the *Speedway News*:

The need for better equipment is still insufficiently appreciated in managerial quarters. The Wembley management recognised the value of fast and reliable machines, but most of their rivals did no more than complain because their own men were less well mounted. The London Motor Sports [the name of Mockford and Smith's company], whose team of excellent riders had been hampered throughout the season by mechanical trouble, engaged a recognised

Each Crystal Palace rider was awarded his own cup by the Supporters' Club to commemorate the team's London Cup win. This is Triss Sharp's.

CRYSTAL PALACE TEAM—LONDON CUP WINNERS, 1931.
Back Row: Jim Cowie, S. Pitcher, Nobby Key, Triss Sharp, Ron Johnson and Tom Farndon.
Front Row: Alf Sawford, Roger Frogley (Capt.), Harry Shepherd and Joe Francis.

The Crystal Palace team featured on the front cover of *Speedway News* after winning the London Cup in 1931. From left to right, back row: Jim Cowie, Bill 'Skid' Pitcher, Nobby Key, Triss Sharp, Ron Johnson, Tom Farndon. Front row: Alf Sawford, Roger Frogley (captain), Harry Shepherd, Joe Francis.

expert to take charge of the well-equipped workshops which were established at the Crystal Palace, and the results have probably exceeded their expectations. We congratulate riders and management alike, and trust the lesson will not be wasted.

Three further victories followed in the next three home matches, 30-22 against Wimbledon, 39-15 against High Beech and 38-15 against Lea Bridge, Farndon and Francis both scoring maximums in the latter two matches. These were the last matches of the season and left Crystal Palace in fourth place with 44 points, just two behind West Ham in third.

The last meeting of the season was to have featured two special attempts on the track record by Johnson and Francis. With the Wallis/J.A.P. machines now showing their superiority over every other type of speedway bike, the J.A.P. manufacturers, J. A. Prestwich Ltd., agreed to send down a special super-tuned engine, which Wallis would then personally install in one of his frames. The expectation was that this bike would be the first in Britain to exceed 50 mph. The current track record at Crystal Palace was held by Colin Watson at a speed of 48.33 mph, so the 50 mph mark was felt to be well within reach of such a super charged bike. Sadly, the J.A.P. motor blew up in practice, so Johnson and Francis had to make two attempts on their own bikes. The best speed was achieved by Francis who recorded 47.33 mph.

By the end of the season, Mockford had managed to persuade Farndon to use the new Wallis/J.A.P. machine and the facilities on offer at the workshops. The result of this was that in two special meetings in October, Farndon equalled the track record at Wembley and broke the track record at Wimbledon.

After a bit of a shaky start, Farndon had got better and better as the season wore on. But not only was he now able to match the best in the country in ability, he was also one of the most spectacular riders around and his never-say-die attitude endeared him to the thousands of Crystal Palace supporters; he was fast becoming their idol.

Just two incidents sum up what made him so popular. In the second half of the programme following the London Cup final at Wembley, Farndon continued to carry all before him. He won the Palace heat of the scratch race event after a hair-raising exhibition when at one point he actually fell and his elbow touched the cinders, but he raised his machine and continued as though nothing had happened, winning the heat from Johnson. He then beat home crowd favourite, Jack Ormston, in the final. And then at the home match against Wimbledon on 4 October, his carburettor came off in one heat and he managed to finish the race by holding it in place.

While Farndon's fortunes were on the up, those of the former star of the Crystal Palace team, and first English Star champion, Roger Frogley, were decidedly on the way down. Although he would sometimes turn in a good performance, he was no longer the rider he had once been. Johnson, Francis and Key continued to ride well for the team, while Shepherd provided good support. Sharp too had his moments, but like Frogley, he was past his best.

Nevertheless, the form of the team as a whole towards the end of the season was just stunning, and if they could keep it up in 1932, there was no doubt they would be in the final reckoning for any trophy going.

At the end of the season, Sharp got married while Key, Frogley and Farndon went off to New Zealand to ride out there with an English team. The Supporters' Club announced that they would be organising weekly dances throughout the winter in the new Crystal Palace dance hall from 7:30 to 11:30 p.m., complete with cabaret and whist drive, to their own cabaret troupe under the leadership of Miss Mary Ugle and the Palace Speedway Revellers Orchestra. 1s 6d for members and 2s 6d for non-members. There were also to be special nights on Armistice Night, Boxing Night, New Year's Eve, St Patrick's Night and Valentine's Night when the doors would be open until 2:00 a.m. Alcoholic beverages, however, were only available until 10:00 p.m.

1931 – Southern League

11 April	H	Lea Bridge	W	31-21
14 April	A	West Ham	L	19-33
18 April	H	Southampton	W	30-24
2 May	H	Wimbledon	W	32-22
9 May	H	Stamford Bridge	W	26-24
12 May	A	Harringay	L	21-30
14 May	A	Wembley	L	12-41
16 May	H	Harringay	W	27-26
20 May	A	Lea Bridge	W	25-23
25 May	A	High Beech	L	23-27
27 May	A	Stamford Bridge	L	21-32
30 May	H	West Ham	L	25-27
4 June	A	Nottingham	L	25-29
6 June	H	Nottingham	W	29-24
20 June	H	Wembley	L	16-36
24 June	A	Southampton	L	18-36

29 June	A	Wimbledon	L	13-40
2 July	A	Coventry	L	25-29
4 July	A	High Beech	L	20-32
4 July	H	High Beech	W	33-20
8 July	A	Belle Vue	L	26-28
11 July	H	Coventry	W	32-20
18 July	H	Wembley	W	30-23
30 July	A	Wembley	L	19-34
1 August	H	Southampton	W	38-15
3 August	A	Stamford Bridge	L	25-28
8 August	H	Stamford Bridge	W	31-23
15 August	H	Coventry	W	36-18
19 August	A	Lea Bridge	W	32-22
2 September	A	Southampton	W	31-21
5 September	H	West Ham	W	32-22
7 September	A	Wimbledon	L	22-31
17 September	A	Coventry	W	35-19
26 September	H	Belle Vue	W	45-9
29 September	A	West Ham	W	28-23
3 October	H	Wimbledon	W	30-22
10 October	H	High Beech	W	39-15
10 October	H	Lea Bridge	W	38-15

National Trophy

First round
Bye

Second round

8 June	A	Wimbledon	L	36-60
13 June	H	Wimbledon	D	48-48

Lost 84-108 on aggregate

London Cup

First round
Bye

Semi final

H	Lea Bridge	W	69-27
A	Lea Bridge	W	55-41

Won 124-68 on aggregate

Final

19 September	H	Wembley	W	59-36
24 September	A	Wembley	W	55-40

Won 114-76 on aggregate

Crystal Palace become London Cup champions

Rider	M	Pts	Ave
Nobby Key	21	115	5.48
Joe Francis	38	195.5	5.14
Ron Johnson	37	186	5.03
Tom Farndon	33	154	4.67
Harry Shepherd	38	164.5	4.33
Roger Frogley	37	143	3.86
Triss Sharp	13	38	2.92
Alf Sawford	6	14	2.33
George Lovick	8	12	1.50

1932

Following the success of the National Trophy in bringing together the teams from the north and the south, the promoters agreed to amalgamate the two leagues into one national league for the 1932 season. There were to be two league competitions during the season, in the first half of the year the clubs would contest the National Speedway Association Trophy, while in the second half the National League itself would be at stake.

Mockford announced the Glaziers' line up with the main six as Johnson, captain, Farndon, Francis, Key, Shepherd and Frogley, with support from Sharp and Sawford. Clem Mitchell had returned and the best of the 1931 juniors, Jim Wilmott was named as a squad member. Jim Cowie and George Dykes were signed up from Nottingham. A Supporters' Club dinner was organised to welcome back Frogley, Farndon and Key on their return from New Zealand.

Fred Mockford (second left) greets Nobby Key (left), Tom Farndon (centre), and Roger Frogley (right) with his wife, Audrey, on the quayside on their arrival back in England following a visit to New Zealand over the winter of 1931-32.

As at the start of 1931, there was a great feeling of optimism that the team would do well this year. With their late season success in the London Cup there were probably more legitimate grounds for hope than the previous year. Johnson, Francis, Farndon and Key were as good a top quartet as any team had. Frogley was also a great rider who, with better equipment, could get back to his old form. The last rider in the regular team, Shepherd, had had an erratic 1931, but certainly had the ability; if he did fail, there were two good riders in Sharp and Mitchell to call on.

The season started well with a 37-16 away victory at Plymouth. Johnson equalled the track record in heat one and then Farndon lowered it by 0.8 seconds in heat four. It was a good all-round solid display.

The home season started on 16 April with Francis clipping 0.8 seconds off Vic Huxley's track record with a time of 78.4. He then won all three of his heats in the league match against Sheffield, which the Glaziers won 36-17. It was a brilliant victory, with the Crystal Palace lads winning every single heat. The only 3-3 of the afternoon was due to Farndon falling while leading heat seven by an enormous distance. Mockford was a little unhappy that

Farndon should be prepared to take such risks while holding a comfortable lead, but accepted that there wasn't much he could do about it by saying 'Tom Farndon cannot go slow'. So easy was the overall victory that Francis deliberately held back at the start of heat nine so that he could make a race of it by carving his way through the field, which he did, to finish in front of his team mate Harry Shepherd.

The Supporters' Club arranged a dinner and concert for 7 May with supporters being urged to bring along sheet music as the band the organisers had hired 'don't have much of their own!'

The start of the season also saw an elimination competition between the league's leading riders to find a challenger for Jack Parker's British Individual Championship. In the first round Farndon was drawn against Wembley's Colin Watson. The first leg was held at Crystal Palace on 23 April and Farndon won 2-0 in such a convincing manner that he smashed Francis's new track record, taking an incredible 1.4 seconds off the time set only the week before. The time of 77 seconds constituted a new record for all British quarter-mile tracks.

In the league match against Plymouth which followed, Farndon also set a new one-lap record on his way to winning heat three when he was timed at 18.6 seconds for one lap. Sadly, after such a magnificent meeting, Farndon was injured in heat seven and had to be taken to hospital. Plymouth's Stan Lupton drifted out near the fence forcing Farndon right out. Practically any other rider would have shut off, but not Farndon, he tried to go through the narrowest of gaps between Lupton and the fence but there was literally no room and he touched the fence turning a terrifying somersault as his machine leapt in to the air landing on him as he lay on the track. There was a deathly hush around the stadium as he was carried off on a stretcher and rushed straight to the Cottage Hospital. Fortunately the accident had looked much worse than it was and Farndon was found to be suffering from nothing more than minor concussion. He was allowed home later in the afternoon.

Farndon's place in the re-run was taken by Frogley who won the race and then announced that this would be his last ride for Crystal Palace, at least for the time being. He felt that he needed a rest to regain some of his former appetite for the sport as his form was still a bit patchy. Crystal Palace won the match 35-19.

Crystal Palace suffered a sensational defeat in their next match – their first of the season – away at Farndon's old stamping ground, Coventry, going down 23-26. The turning point came in heat five when both Crystal Palace riders – Francis and Shepherd – fell. In fact the main cause of the Glaziers' defeat against unlikely Coventry was the number of times they fell during the match.

Harry 'Shep' Shepherd, who first proposed the idea of a starting gate, rode for Crystal Palace from 1930 to 1933.

After a disastrous start to the next meeting when Johnson and Francis collided during the pre-match grand parade causing so much damage to the captain's bike that he finished last in his first race, Crystal Palace recovered to inflict on Wembley their first defeat of the season. The hero of the match for the Glaziers turned out to be Nobby Key who scored a perfect maximum. The final score of 27-26 was enough to return Crystal Palace to the top of the table.

A 31-23 win over Southampton at home with Farndon suffering engine failure in all three of his heats saw Key score his second successive maximum. His form was such that he was now beginning to eclipse Johnson and Farndon as the star of the Crystal Palace outfit.

The Southampton match was followed in the second half by a 15-8 London Reserves' League match win over Stamford Bridge. The team for this encounter was Sharp, Mitchell, Wilmott and an 18-year-old youngster by the name of George Newton, who scored 5 paid 6 from his two rides.

Meanwhile, the Supporters' Club were able to announce that they were expecting their 5,000[th] member at any moment.

In the return leg of the British Individual Championship first round qualifier, Farndon beat Watson on the latter's home track of Wembley. Farndon equalled the Wembley track record of 77.4 seconds in doing so.

Four days after the Southampton match, Crystal Palace travelled north to visit Sheffield. At this point in the season, the Glaziers had lost just one match and were equal top of the table with Wimbledon, while Sheffield had so far failed to win a single match. The result seemed to be a foregone conclusion, but in one of the biggest upsets of all time, Sheffield absolutely pulverised Crystal Palace, defeating them by the overwhelming margin of 22 points at 38-16. It was said that the track was very bumpy and that the Crystal Palace riders did not want to take any undue risks. The Glaziers only heat winner was Farndon who won heat six. He and Francis were Crystal Palace's top scorers with four each.

This defeat was followed by another big loss, this time at home, as the Glaziers went down 18-36 to Stamford Bridge. The Crystal Palace heat leaders had no answer to the Pensioners' top three of Frank Arthur, Dick Smythe and Arthur Warwick.

One of the main noticeable aspects contributing to Crystal Palace's decline in fortunes was that they no longer enjoyed the technical superiority over the other teams that had taken them to success in the latter half of the previous season. Having seen the results that paying attention to the bikes could bring, many of the other teams in the league were now instituting workshops of their own and getting in top-class mechanics to look after their machines as well.

Crystal Palace needed to do something to halt this slide in their fortunes; in their next match away at Wimbledon it was their turn to provide the three match winners in Farndon, Francis and Key, with Farndon being easily the best rider on view, defeating the great Vic Huxley on his own track. The 29-25 victory was just the pick-me-up the team needed.

They followed this up with a good 35-18 victory over Coventry, taking full revenge for their defeat earlier in the season. Both Johnson and Farndon scored maximums and Shepherd had his best match for some time, contributing seven points.

Three Palace riders were selected for the first Test match held on 4 June at Stamford Bridge; Farndon and Key for England and Johnson for Australia. Australia was expected to win the match, but they had reckoned without Farndon, the hero of the night, who top scored with 11 points. Key added 6 points to England's total of 50, while Johnson scored four of Australia's 41.

Roger Frogley returned for the Glaziers' next match against Wembley, but his poor showing of only two points from three rides convinced him that he wasn't ready to return, and he decided to pack it in for the season. Farndon won two heats but had a puncture in his third while leading. Strangely, Ormston, who was second at the time, also had a puncture. The final score was Wembley 32 Crystal Palace 22.

The young George Newton caused a major sensation in his next London Reserves' League outing at West Ham. With one heat to go, Crystal Palace led by a single point. Newton was up against West Ham's Les Wootton and Tommy Price. As the riders approached the start, Newton flew off with his throttle wide open, keeping it that way for the whole four laps. In an amazing ride for the 18-year-old first-year novice, he managed to equal Vic Huxley's two-year-old track record of 82.8 seconds.

On 12 June the Crystal Palace Supporters' Club arranged a day's outing to the Frogleys' Annual Air Pageant at their Broxbourne airfield. Fred Mockford took an active part in the proceedings by making a parachute descent.

The young George Newton, another spectacular leg trailer in the Tom Farndon mould, rode for Crystal Palace in 1932 and 1933.

In view of their recent patchy form and Frogley's definite decision to quit at least for the season, Mockford decided to revamp the team and to change the pairings. Triss Sharp came back to partner Farndon, while the match winning combination of previous seasons, Johnson and Francis, was restored. The third pairing was Key and Shepherd.

The new-look team proceeded to a comfortable victory over West Ham, winning 33-21. The only opposition came from Bluey Wilkinson, who rode brilliantly, but even he met his match in Farndon in heat seven.

In the return match at Custom House three days later, Crystal Palace looked to have the beating of the Hammers until the seventh heat. At the end of the sixth heat they led by 6 points, but in heat seven neither Palace rider managed to finish the race as Johnson's chain broke and Francis hit a rough patch which momentarily jerked him over the white line, causing him to be excluded. In heat eight, Key and Newton, the latter making his senior team debut, got mixed up with each other on the first bend, causing both of them to fall. Newton managed to remount but had no chance of catching the two West Ham riders. So in the space of two heats, Crystal Palace had gone from 6 points up to 3 behind with just one heat to go. The last heat turned into a bit of a farce, as first of all Farndon fell on the first corner and then Croombs had an engine failure while in the lead. Farndon meantime had remounted and was chasing after Spinks and teammate Shepherd. Finally Shepherd also packed up with engine failure, leaving Spinks to come home ahead of Farndon for a 3-2 to West Ham win, and a final 28-24 victory for the Hammers.

The year's first interim league averages were published on 11 June and they showed that Nobby Key was, somewhat surprisingly, the top Crystal Palace rider with a 68.6 per cent average. Overall he stood in 8th place. Farndon was in 11th place with 66.6 per cent, while Francis was 18th with 59.4 per cent.

Meanwhile Farndon's pursuit of being named challenger for Parker's British Individual Championship continued with a 2-1 victory over Frank Arthur at the latter's home track, Stamford Bridge. With it looking likely that Farndon would progress to the final elimination round against Eric Langton, Arthur pulled off a shock win at Crystal Palace and the tie had to go to a decider at Plymouth, where Arthur once again got the better of Farndon.

The return of the Johnson/Francis pairing played a significant role in the Glaziers' next victory, away at the strongly fancied Belle Vue. Their top pairing, Eric Langton and Frank Varey, was usually regarded as the strongest in the league, but in heat one, and on their own track, they had to give best to Johnson and Francis who took a 5-1 off them. With Farndon also in top form, Crystal Palace took the match 29-24.

The following week, Crystal Palace did even better against Belle Vue, beating them 33-18 back at Sydenham. Francis and Key both scored maximums, while Newton had his best meeting so far, scoring five points.

Towards the end of June, Sheffield withdrew from the league and Crystal Palace was able to sign up two of their riders, Eric Blain and Alec Peel.

Two more victories followed: 32-22 away at Clapton, who had taken over Southampton's fixtures, and 37-17 at home to Wimbledon. The wobbly patch that Crystal Palace had experienced earlier in the season seemed to be behind them and although the National Association Trophy league title now seemed beyond them, they were hopeful that they were running into form just in time for the start of the National League itself.

The following meeting at Sydenham saw the Crystal Palace round of the Star Rider's Championship. As in 1931, all teams were allowed two riders in the final, one to come through a qualifying process at their own track, the other to be nominated by the club. The first heat of the first round was won by Alec Peel from Jim Willmott, while the second was won by Harry Shepherd from Triss Sharp. The third heat brought together the three crowd favourites, Johnson, Francis and Farndon, and was eagerly anticipated by the crowd. Disappointingly, Farndon fell on the first bend but the other two raced neck and neck until Johnson overslid on the last corner of the last lap. Although he corrected the slide, he had lost too much ground and Francis went on to win the heat.

The first semi-final saw Francis defeat Shepherd, while the second saw Johnson push Peel into second place. Therefore the final was more or less a re-run of the third heat, and once again it was a shoulder to shoulder affair until Johnson's front tyre punctured, leaving Francis to come home alone and become one of Crystal Palace's representatives in the Star Riders' Championship final.

Crystal Palace's last match in the National Association Trophy league was against Stamford Bridge, the team that had already done enough to win it. The match at Stamford Bridge's Chelsea track was one of the most exciting seen that season, with passing and repassing in practically every heat. As befitting his new status as the Glaziers' representative in the Star Riders' Final, Francis was the pick of the Crystal Palace riders, scoring seven points, but it wasn't enough to prevent Stamford Bridge from winning 30-24.

At the end of the first half of the season, Crystal Palace finished third in the league behind Stamford Bridge and Wembley, while in the averages, their top rider, Nobby Key, was also third with an average of 73.5 per cent behind

Wimbledon's Dick Case (81.5 per cent) and Belle Vue's Eric Langton (76.1 per cent).

The Glaziers began the National League campaign proper with a narrow 26-25 away victory at West Ham. The team had high hopes of performing well in the new league with a strong line-up consisting of Johnson, Farndon, Francis, Key, Blain and Newton, who had shown astonishing progress in the first half of the year. And sure enough, even without Johnson and Farndon who were away on Test duty, Crystal Palace scored an easy home victory over Plymouth, 31-20, in their first home match. Johnson and Farndon's places were taken by two Crystal Palace stalwarts, Harry Shepherd and Triss Sharp.

The Glaziers then set out to retain their London Cup title with a good two-leg victory over Clapton, winning both legs with Ron Johnson proving invincible home and away. Another match, another trophy, as Crystal Palace then took on and beat Wimbledon in the National Trophy second round, first leg.

It was back to National League action next with a trip up to Manchester to take on the might of Belle Vue. Sadly, apart from Farndon, the Glaziers were outridden by a strong Aces team, losing 22-32. Alec Peel made his first team debut for Crystal Palace in this match but suffered spinal injuries after crashing in heat four.

Another view of the Crystal Palace track from the opposite side to that shown on p. 43.

The Crystal Palace Test match followed, with three of the home track riders representing their respective countries. Unfortunately, Farndon injured his leg in his first ride and only managed four points while Johnson had a poor afternoon and scored just five. The best of the trio was Key, who, despite scoring only six points, recorded the fastest time of the night.

In spite of his injuries at Belle Vue just nine days earlier, Peel turned out once again for the Glaziers on 10 August and proved to be a somewhat surprising match winner, recording a maximum 9 points in Crystal Palace's fine 29-25 away win over the National Association Trophy winners, Stamford Bridge, who suffered their first home defeat of the year.

The Glaziers put up a spirited fight in the second leg of their National Trophy tie against Wimbledon to try and hold on to their 8-point advantage from the first leg. But they came up against a strong Dons team with both Vic Huxley and Dick Case proving unbeatable. Going into the last heat they were still only 2 points behind on aggregate, but Case shot away from the start and never looked like being beaten. The final aggregate score was Wimbledon 97 Crystal Palace 93.

Following an unexpected home defeat at the hands of West Ham, 25-27, Crystal Palace's next outing was the semi-final of the London Cup, with the Glaziers out to retain their trophy against a strong Wembley side. Sadly, the Glaziers were well off the pace in the first leg at the Empire Stadium as the rampant Lions crushed them 65-30. To add insult to injury, Wembley's Ginger Lees also broke Farndon's track record in heat two. In an effort to get back his track record, Farndon overdid it in heat twelve and got into a big overslide. Suddenly the grip returned but he was so far sideways that he shot straight onto the centre green and out of the race.

Back home in Sydenham, the Glaziers set about retrieving the 35-point deficit from the first leg. By the time of the interval after heat eight, it looked as though they might even do it. With Johnson and Francis unbeaten and Peel and Farndon only dropping 1 point the score was 32-15 or 62-80 on aggregate. But Wembley staged a minor comeback in the second half and although Crystal Palace ran out winners on the night, 56-37, Wembley held on to their lead and were through to the final, 102-86. Johnson had been the Glaziers' hero in both legs, scoring 22 points out of a possible 24, but it meant their one and only trophy had now gone.

In spite of losing their grip on the London Cup, Crystal Palace were continuing to have a good run in the National League and following a 31-22 away victory over Coventry and a 34-20 demolition of Wimbledon at Sydenham, they found themselves in third place just 4 points behind the leaders, Wembley, at the end of August.

Heat seven of the Wimbledon encounter saw two false starts. On the second occasion, the Wimbledon captain, Vic Huxley, was warned by the steward and excluded. Huxley felt strongly that he had done nothing wrong and asked one of the ambulance men to take a message to the steward that he would like him to come down so he could speak to him. The steward refused to leave his box and Huxley refused to get off the track. Eventually the steward did come down and the two men met in the middle of the track. After a short conversation, the steward agreed to allow Huxley back in the race. As soon as the race started Huxley had engine failure.

Two more big victories for Crystal Palace followed: 35-19 at home to Clapton and the same score away at Plymouth, Johnson scoring a maximum in both matches.

On 24 September, Crystal Palace met Wembley at home. At this point, the Glaziers had lost two matches, while Wembley had lost just one, so this match was vital to Crystal Palace's hopes of taking the league title. In fact, by this stage of the season, Crystal Palace was the only team capable of stopping Wembley from taking the title.

The match started well for the home side, with Johnson and Francis taking a 5-1, but it was not without incident, as befitted a match of such importance. Wembley's Wally Kilmister fell and then remounted. However, he waited until Johnson, who was leading the race, came round and then set off hard just in front of him, racing him but nearly a lap behind in the hope that he could slow him up to allow his team mate, Jack Ormston, to catch and pass him. But the 'professional foul' didn't work, and Kilmister dropped out when he was eventually lapped. Heats two and three went the other way as Wembley struck back with two 4-2s, making the scores level after three heats. Heat four saw a severe setback for the Glaziers as Wembley's Jack Ormston and Wally Kilmister took a 5-1 over Key and Sawford. Crystal Palace returned the favour in heat five as Farndon shot into the lead from Van Praag and Watson, with Peel struggling in last place. Suddenly, Peel seemed to find an extra turn of speed and fought his way past both his Wembley opponents, bringing the match back to level pegging with four heats to go.

The next race looked as though it could be the decider as the only two unbeaten riders on each side – Johnson and Lees – met. The tension in the stadium was almost unbearable as the riders rode round to the start, but it was declared a false start. As if to emphasise the importance of the race there were several more false starts before the steward allowed the riders to go, with Lees taking the lead in to the first bend, hotly pursued by Johnson. Two or three times, the Crystal Palace captain tried to dive through, but each time he was blocked by Lees. On the last bend of the last lap, Johnson just left everything turned on, and to the wild cheering of the crowd, swept round the outside, just passing Lees on the run in to win by inches. However, with Gordon Byers taking third place, the match was still in the balance.

Farndon won heat seven comfortably, but behind him there was a neck-and-neck duel between Peel and Ormston, with the Wembley rider just getting the better of the home team rider. Nevertheless, it was a 4-2 for Crystal Palace, putting them in front by two points. The next race was to prove decisive as Johnson and Francis were just too good for Van Praag and Watson, and led them from start to finish. Just for good measure, Sharp, who was brought in as a reserve in place of Sawford, rubbed salt in to the wounds in the last heat by beating Lees. The final score in this vital league match was Crystal Palace 30 Wembley 24. It now meant that both teams had lost two matches and the championship was wide open.

Crystal Palace followed up this magnificent performance with another victory, this time over Coventry, with Johnson scoring his fourth successive league maximum.

Although Johnson scored yet another maximum in the away fixture at Clapton, the Glaziers were surprisingly beaten, 28-26. However, the Crystal Palace management protested at the result because of the number of bad starts that were allowed, and the Control Board agreed to a re-run. However, it didn't do them any good as they lost the replay by almost the same score, 28-25. The main difference this time was that Johnson only scored 5 points while Farndon top scored with 6 paid 7.

With the loss at Clapton, Crystal Palace's next match away at Wembley was absolutely crucial. Both teams had lost three matches but Wembley only had one further match after the Crystal Palace match and were four points ahead of the Glaziers, who had another three matches to race, including fixtures against strong opponents in Stamford Bridge and Belle Vue. Coming up to the last heat the scores were level at 24 all. At the start, Farndon flew into a commanding lead, but with Greenwood and Kilmister filling the minor places, it looked as though the final result would be a draw, good enough to still give the Glaziers a chance at the league championship.

The Crystal Palace contingent, who numbered in their hundreds, were on their feet shouting themselves hoarse as Farndon continued to increase his lead. But suddenly the shouting died as, dramatically, Farndon overdid it on the last lap and fell, leaving the two Wembley riders to take the chequered flag for a 5-1, giving Wembley the match, 29-25, and most probably, the league championship. In fact, Wembley wrapped up the league that evening by beating Coventry in the second part of a double header.

Crystal Palace's last three matches resulted in two wins, one away at Wimbledon and one at home to Belle Vue, and a draw at home to Stamford Bridge.

Although they had missed out on the league, it was a very creditable performance for the Glaziers, coming runners-up in the league in front of much more fancied teams such as Stamford Bridge and Belle Vue. The good performance was due mainly to the consistency of the three heat leaders, Johnson, Key and Farndon, all recording plus six averages. Johnson, in particular, had a brilliant patch towards the end of the season, scoring six maximums out of the last nine matches. With every reason to suppose that these three riders could improve even further, there were high hopes for 1933.

1932 – National Association Trophy

12 April	A	Plymouth	W	37-16
16 April	H	Sheffield	W	36-17
23 April	H	Plymouth	W	35-19
28 April	A	Coventry	L	23-26
30 April	H	Wembley	W	27-26
7 May	H	Southampton	W	31-23*
11 May	A	Sheffield	L	16-38
14 May	H	Stamford Bridge	L	18-36
16 May	A	Wimbledon	W	29-25
21 May	H	Coventry	W	35-18
2 June	A	Wembley	L	22-32
11 June	H	West Ham	W	33-21
14 June	A	West Ham	L	24-28
18 June	A	Belle Vue	W	29-24
25 June	H	Belle Vue	W	34-18
29 June	A	Clapton	W	32-22*
2 July	H	Wimbledon	W	37-17
9 July	A	Stamford Bridge	L	24-30

*Southampton moved to Clapton during the season

1932 – National League

12 July	A	West Ham	W	26-25
16 July	H	Plymouth	W	31-20

1 August	A	Belle Vue	L	22-32
10 August	A	Stamford Bridge	W	29-25
13 August	H	West Ham	L	25-27
25 August	A	Coventry	W	31-22
27 August	H	Wimbledon	W	34-20
13 September	A	Plymouth	W	35-19
17 September	H	Clapton	W	35-19
24 September	H	Wembley	W	30-24
1 October	H	Coventry	W	31-22
5 October	A	Clapton	L	25-28*
6 October	A	Wembley	L	25-29
10 October	A	Wimbledon	W	31-23
15 October	H	Stamford Bridge	D	27-27
22 October	H	Belle Vue	W	30-24

* Replay of match

National Trophy

First round
Bye

Second round

| A | Coventry | L | 41-55 |
| H | Coventry | W | 50-44 |

Lost 91-99 on aggregate

London Cup

First round

| H | Clapton | W | 54-42 |
| A | Clapton | W | 48-42 |

Won 102-84 on aggregate

Semi final

| A | Wembley | L | 30-65 |
| H | Wembley | W | 56-37 |

Lost 86-102 on aggregate

National Association Trophy

Rider	M	Pts	Ave
Nobby Key	18	114	6.33
Tom Farndon	18	104	5.78
Joe Francis	18	103	5.72
Ron Johnson	17	79	4.68
Harry Shepherd	18	59	3.28
Alf Sawford	10	26	2.60
Triss Sharp	8	15	1.88

National League

Rider	M	Pts	Ave
Ron Johnson	15	103	6.87
Nobby Key	15	99	6.60
Tom Farndon	15	91	6.07
Joe Francis	16	73	4.56
Eric Blain	7	23	3.29
Triss Sharp	6	14	2.33
Alec Peel	13	30	2.31
Alf Sawford	6	12	2.00
Harry Shepherd	9	15	1.67

1933

Before the 1933 season began, Blain was transferred to Sheffield and Peel to Coventry. Mockford announced that the regular line up of his team would be Johnson, Farndon, Francis, Key, Shepherd, Newton and Sharp. He also said that he had discovered a new junior rider by the name of Les Gregory, for whom he had high hopes. He was said to have a style reminiscent of Johnson.

Key's appearance in the team was dependant on his signing a new contract introduced by the Control Board for 1933. The new contracts introduced for riders spending their winter abroad was part of an attempt to introduce a form of rider control so that some teams did not get too powerful. Accordingly it was announced that any rider not in the country over the close season, even if they appeared on a team's retained list, would become the property of the

Control Board and could be allocated to any team on their return. As Key had spent the winter in Australia, he came into this category and he was asked to sign a new contract by the Control Board. Key was not happy about this as he wished to stay at Sydenham and refused to sign the new contract. He was given until the end of May by the Control Board to sign the new contract or face suspension. Until then he was allowed to continue as a Crystal Palace rider.

Johnson started the season as he had finished the previous one with a 9-point maximum in a challenge match at home to Wimbledon.

This was the last time a rider would be able to score a 9-point maximum that season as point scoring reverted to that used in 1929, i.e. 4 for a win, 2 for a second and 1 for a third. Other changes to occur in 1933 were the abolition of the National Speedway Association Trophy, with the National League extended so that each team raced every other team twice home and twice away, and a new method of starting races. In spite of a number of changes to the starting procedure, the rolling start was still causing many problems with many false starts and many races having to be restarted. The new method meant that riders would no longer have to ride one lap of the track, but would come up to the line and stop; the race would then be started on a clutch start by the steward signalling with a green light instead of a flag.

The 1933 Crystal Palace National League team. From left to right: Triss Sharp, Joe Francis, Nobby Key, Fred Mockford (manager, standing), Ron Johnson (captain), Tom Farndon, Harry 'Shep' Shepherd, George Newton.

The Glaziers' opening league match of the season was away at West Ham. Once again, Johnson was the star of the show for Crystal Palace, scoring two wins and unluckily falling in his other ride. Sadly, he did not receive much backing from the rest of the team, as they went down 36-24. Four days later it was an altogether different team that crushed the Hammers 41-21 in the return fixture. Francis scored a maximum, while both Johnson and Key lost to just one opponent each. But perhaps the biggest cheer of the night was reserved for old stalwart, Triss Sharp, who won his last heat after Bluey Wilkinson had been excluded for continuing to push start past the forward foul line.

It looked as though the Glaziers had returned to the sort of form that made them runners-up in 1932 as they went in to a 10-point lead away at League Champions, Wembley, in their next match. The first four heats were all won by Crystal Palace riders, with the highlights being heat one, when Johnson passed Lees on the inside on the last bend much to the latter's surprise, and heat three, when Shepherd and Farndon scored a 6-1 over their opponents.

Although heat four was won by Francis by a big margin, it was really the turning point of the match. There had been more than one instance of riders trying to anticipate the start. It happened again in heat four as Johnson shot off a fraction of a second before the green light went on and was excluded for his transgression. The Palace team were a little aggrieved at this exclusion as they felt the Wembley riders had been getting away with jumping the start in the first three races and they had had to win them all the hard way, coming from behind. In heat five Key got a very poor start while Newton suffered mechanical problems and didn't start at all. Although Key got past the two Wembley riders, he fell while leading and, although he remounted, it was a 6-1 to Wembley. In the next heat, both Shepherd and Farndon were left at the start, resulting in another 6-1 to Wembley. Johnson stopped the rot in heat seven, winning comfortably, but a mix up in heat eight led to Key laying down his machine to avoid hitting Newton, who had become entangled with a Wembley rider. In the end, Crystal Palace's 10-point lead was reversed to a 5-point victory for Wembley, 34-29.

Once again, the Glaziers bounced back at home, overwhelming Wimbledon, 42-21. Sharp was once again the hero with 10 points. The following week, Crystal Palace scored an even easier victory over Sheffield, 49-11. Johnson recorded a full maximum, Farndon a paid maximum and Sharp, 10 points. Sharp was enjoying a real renaissance in form, and in spite of the defeat at Wembley, there was a definite feeling in the Sydenham air that they now had a team capable of carrying off the league title. It was hard to see any weak links and any one of the seven was capable of scoring a maximum on his day.

Crystal Palace *v*. Wembley, 1933. Nobby Key leads from Wembley's Gordon Byers with Ron Johnson in third place.

Sure enough, another big victory followed away at Nottingham. This was the opening meeting at the Lace Town track and after a ceremonial opening by the Lord Mayor of Nottingham, the Glaziers set about their opponents in no uncertain manner, winning by 38 points to 24. And, as if to prove the point that any one of them could score a maximum, it was Harry Shepherd's turn to come up with the goods.

Following yet another stunning victory, this time 40-20 over Clapton, Crystal Palace ran into problems with Nobby Key and Tom Farndon. Key's refusal to sign the overseas contract at the beginning of the season reared its head, and on 30 May, the management put out a press statement: 'Nobby Key, the Palace rider was withdrawn from the Palace team to visit Plymouth tonight owing to the Speedway Control Board having notified the Palace promoter, Mr F. E. Mockford, that Key had refused to sign his contract with the clause concerning overseas riding embodied in same, and as his time expired on Monday for the signing of the contract, he cannot be used for League racing until an agreement has been reached.'

As if that wasn't bad enough, Mockford also announced that Tom Farndon had applied for a transfer to Wembley. He had refused the request for two reasons: firstly, he did not want to lose him, and secondly, even if he did leave, he thought Wembley would be far too strong with Farndon in their line-up as well as all their other stars. If he really wanted to leave, Mockford said he would allow him to go back to Coventry or any of the other weaker provincial tracks. Fortunately, following further discussions between rider and promoter, Farndon agreed to stay, but a solution was not so easily attainable for Key's position as he steadfastly refused to sign the new contract.

Because of the uncertain situation, neither Key nor Farndon took part in the match at Plymouth, the result of which was a narrow defeat for Crystal Palace by 33 points to 30. Their places were taken by two untried juniors in Eric Hustwayte and Jack Riddle. Newton and Sharp were the Glaziers' top scorers with 10 and 8 respectively.

Following this match, the ever-popular Triss Sharp was transferred to Coventry, thus ending a long association with Crystal Palace which went back to the path racing days before the speedway had even arrived.

Although Farndon quickly returned to the saddle for the Glaziers, the two incidents seemed to have unsettled the team as they were overwhelmed by Belle Vue, 45-14. It was just as well that Farndon had settled his differences as he was the only Crystal Palace rider to win a heat, and finished with 8 points altogether. The next highest scorers were Francis and Riddle with just 2 points each. Heat seven was one of the strangest races seen all season. Both Newton and Belle Vue's Dixon were disqualified for starting infringements, leaving just Johnson and Kitchen to start the race. They collided before they had gone 10 yards and the race was restarted. Johnson was too badly injured to be able to take part in the re-run and his place was taken by Hustwayte, but he also fell and Kitchen motored round alone for a 4-0.

Although Crystal Palace was not doing as well away from home as they would have wished, they were still racking up the points on their own track, and they crushed Coventry 44-18. In fact the Crystal Palace riders were so superior to their Coventry counterparts that towards the end of the match they were deliberately hanging back at the start to liven up the proceedings by having to come from the back. Farndon and Johnson both scored maximums, while the Francis/Shepherd pairing did not drop a point.

Although he was not quite the force he had been at the end of the previous season, Johnson was chosen to take part in the eliminating contest for the vacant British Individual Championship, following Eric Langton's resignation of the title. His first opponent was Wembley's Wally Kilmister. Johnson won both legs, 2-0 at Wembley and 2-1 at Crystal Palace.

Although the new clutch start had been introduced in an effort to overcome the problems with false starts, the system still wasn't working very well as riders were still edging forward and trying to anticipate the start. On 17 June, following the match against Nottingham, which the Glaziers won 41-22, Fred Mockford, together with Harry Shepherd, tried out yet another new starting technique aimed at cutting out the recalled starts and disqualifications. Borrowed from horse racing, it was an extremely simple idea consisting of a frame extended across the track with three horizontal tapes which rise as an operator pulls the handle; in other words, a starting gate. There were no springs or complicated machinery of any kind to go wrong, the motive power being supplied by gravity through the medium of a weight. Before the experiment took place, there was a fear that the riders would continually breast the tapes and the starting gate would prove to be no better than any other system in stopping false starts. However, the starting method that was employed prevented this happening as the riders had to line up a foot behind the gate with their engines running and their clutches out and start as soon as the tapes rose. Because of the speed of the tapes rising, no-one was able to anticipate the start. It was claimed that the presence of something tangible in front of them prevented the riders from jumping off before the tapes rose, and all the riders who took part in the experiment spoke strongly in favour of the starting gate. Although the experiment was an undoubted success, fears were expressed that speedway riders were such an ingenious lot that it would not be long before they found a way to anticipate the tapes and still manage to get flyers.

In spite of these doubts, the Control Board announced at its meeting the following Tuesday that it had been so impressed by the results of the

Tom Farndon, left, and Harry Shepherd give the new starting gate a trial while Nobby Key looks on behind.

experiment at Crystal Palace, it had decided the starting gate was to be installed at all tracks for the purpose of clutch-start racing within three weeks of the date of the notice, and that from then on its use was obligatory in all official fixtures. The only difference to the Crystal Palace experiment was that riders were to line up two feet behind the gate instead of one foot. Any rider touching the tapes would be sent back, and if they repeated the offence they would be excluded from the race. The Control Board added that they couldn't see any reason why all tracks should not be able to install them within three weeks as the cost of constructing the gate was less than £5 including labour charges.

The Glaziers continued to dominate proceedings at home and the following week they even managed to outclass Wembley. This match, held on 23 June, was the first league match in which the starting gate was used. It also saw the return of Nobby Key, who had agreed to sign the contract while the Control Board for their part agreed that he could stay at Crystal Palace. Along with Francis and Farndon he scored 10 points in the 39-23 victory. Use of the starting gate seemed to have a beneficial effect on the speed of races, and in spite of a heavy track due to a continuous downpour earlier on, Joe Francis managed to break the track record for a four-lap clutch start with a time of 84.0 seconds. There was only one incident during the evening of the tapes being touched by a rider, and apart from that, all races were started without any problems.

The following week, Johnson took on Claude Rye in the final of the British Individual Championship. After beating him 2-1 at Wimbledon, Johnson received a walk-over at Crystal Palace as Rye had broken a leg in a crash. Johnson therefore became British Individual Champion. Although, in general, his riding had not quite reached the heights of the previous season, it was, nevertheless, a well-deserved honour for the Crystal Palace captain who had maintained a consistently high standard ever since his first appearance at the club back in 1928.

Crystal Palace set out to regain their *Evening News* London Cup trophy next with a 65-60 away win at Wimbledon. The hero of the night was Joe Francis, who scored a maximum 18 points. Although it was a good away victory by 5 points, the Glaziers were, in fact, leading by 10 points going into the last heat, and looked like extending their lead. Farndon and Newton led in to the first bend, but coming out of the second bend, Newton accidentally ran into Farndon and jammed his footrest under his partner's exhaust pipe, bringing them both to a standstill. Farndon just managed to extricate himself before he was lapped and got round for third place and 1 point.

Another big away victory at Sheffield followed with Francis once again being instrumental in the Glaziers' success, this time scoring another maximum in the 40-23 win.

For the fifth match running, Francis totted up double figures in the next home match with a paid maximum. This time he was joined by Farndon and Shepherd with full maximums in the complete demolition of Plymouth, 45-17.

Amazingly, the brilliant run came to a juddering halt in the second leg of the London Cup tie against Wimbledon. With their 5-point lead from Plough Lane it looked odds-on that the Glaziers would progress through to the semi finals of the cup, but they were in for a rude shock as Wimbledon ended Crystal Palace's undefeated run at home with a stunning 77-49 victory. The turning point came in heat nine as Farndon and Wimbledon's Wal Phillips raced shoulder to shoulder, inseparable for almost the whole 4 laps, until Phillips found a little extra on the last bend to win by about six lengths. For some reason Palace seemed to lose heart after that and the Dons took full control of the match. Francis's good run came to an end after falling in the first heat and he only managed to score 6 points from his six rides.

Although they were now out of the London Cup, Crystal Palace bounced back in their next league fixture, an away tie at West Ham. Although the Hammers' captain, Tiger Stevenson, equalled the track record in the first heat, the Glaziers promptly won the next four, and the score after heat five was West Ham 13 Crystal Palace 22. By the end of the match they had extended that lead to 11 points, winning 37-26. This time it was Key who was the hero, scoring a 12-point maximum.

Crystal Palace then defeated West Ham in the first round of the National Trophy by winning 69-55 at West Ham, with Francis scoring a 24-point maximum and Johnson 20 points with one fall. A 63-63 draw back at Sydenham gave the Glaziers an aggregate 132-188 victory. Stevenson broke the track record in heat one at Crystal Palace by a full second, setting the new time at 81.2, the fastest speed ever recorded in Great Britain for a four-lap clutch-start race.

With riders like Francis, now back to his old form, and Shepherd to back up Johnson, Farndon and Key, Crystal Palace were being touted as possibly the strongest team in the league, at least on a par with the great Belle Vue side; certainly the results, in general, apart from the slight blip against Wimbledon in the London Cup, were supporting this theory. Indeed, such was their strength and depth of talent that they won their next home match against Sheffield even without Johnson and Farndon who were both on Test duty that night at Belle Vue. Once again, Francis, who was acting as captain for the night, turned in a maximum, while Eric Hustwayte, promoted into the team proper for the first time, recorded his first win in Crystal Palace colours. Even the reserve, Lew Lancaster, scored a creditable 3 points from his three rides, which included one fall. The win put the Glaziers up into second place in the league, 4 points behind Belle Vue.

Francis received his due reward when he was chosen to ride for England in the third Test match on his own track along with Farndon. Johnson was once again selected for Australia. Although, in this elite company, Francis only managed 6½ points, he did have the honour of dead heating for first place in heat five with the great Vic Huxley. In fact, he did enough to impress the selectors and was chosen to ride for England in the fourth Test at Wimbledon as well. Farndon scored 11 and Johnson 9 in England's narrow 1-point win against Australia, 63.5-62.5.

At the end of July, the National League averages showed that Francis was in eleventh place with 59.8 per cent; Farndon was sixth with 67.9 per cent and Johnson was in twentieth with 50.8 per cent.

A win for the Glaziers in their next match was vital if they were to take the league title; it was away at Belle Vue, the current league leaders and greatest rivals for top spot honours. So important was the match that 30,000 people attended, including a sizeable contingent from South London, who travelled all the way up to Manchester on a Monday, hopeful of seeing their team draw a step closer to the league title. Although the match was in doubt until the last heat, sadly it was not to be. The Glaziers put up a magnificent showing against one of the greatest teams in the history of the sport, which included in their line-up great names such as Eric Langton, Frank Varey, Max Grosskreautz, Bill Kitchen and Joe Abbot. With one heat to go, Belle Vue led 30-26. A last heat 6-1 for Crystal Palace could still have given them the match. The line-up was Abbot and Kitchen for the Aces with Farndon and Newton for the Glaziers. To the cheers of their own supporters, the Belle Vue pair gated first, but they were hotly pursued by Farndon and Newton. What then took place was one of the best races seen all season and a worthy contest to possibly decide the league championship. Farndon and Newton tried every way they could to get past, and on the very last bend, Farndon swept round the Belle Vue pair to take the chequered flag in a thoroughly deserved victory. Sadly, however, Newton was unable to follow him round and the resulting 4-3 clinched the victory for Belle Vue by just 3 points at 33-30. Once again, both Farndon and Francis had put up tremendous performances, Farndon scoring 9 points and Francis 8.

Two more emphatic wins followed: 37-21 at home to Nottingham, and 34-26 away at Coventry. A strange incident occurred in the latter match when,

Ron Johnson won the British Match Race Championship by defeating Wimbledon's Claude Rye in June and July 1933. He then became the first man in the history of the championship to retain the title when he beat Wimbledon's Syd Jackson over three legs in August of the same year.

following two stoppages for injury, heat four was postponed and run after heat eight, quite contrary to ACU rules.

Johnson's good individual run was continuing as he beat off Syd Jackson, the first challenger for his British Individual Match Race title, and also qualified, along with Tom Farndon, as one of the Crystal Palace representatives in the Star Riders' Championship final.

The team, however, suffered a set-back, losing their National Trophy semi-final tie against Wembley. The damage was done in the first leg at the Empire Stadium as the Lions scored a resounding 77-48 victory. Overall, the Glaziers lost 140-110 on aggregate.

Back in league action on 26 August, Crystal Palace scored a sensational 46-17 victory over Wimbledon. Both Farndon and Francis scored maximums, with the ride of the day belonging to Francis who had a brilliant win over Vic Huxley in heat 7, passing him around the outside on the last bend after an exciting four-lap battle.

The league match against West Ham the next week caused a small riot when a group of spectators invaded the Pavilion following a disputed last heat which led to a narrow 2-point victory for the Hammers. There was an immediate protest by the Crystal Palace management at the way the race was started. After their next meeting, the Control Board issued a statement which said, 'The Speedway Control Board have considered the Crystal Palace protest against the start of the last heat of their league match against West Ham on Saturday last, and have decided that the operation of the starting gate in that race was not in accordance with the regulations and the best interests of the sport. They consider that in fairness to the two teams there is no alternative but to declare last Saturday's match null and void and that it be replayed at the earliest opportunity.'

Coming up to the last heat the score was 29-26 in favour of the Glaziers. As the gate came down, one of the two tapes (one was missing) was seen to be hanging down. When the gate went up, the loose tape caught round George Newton's neck. Farndon, under the impression that a re-start would be ordered, sat still. However, the steward let it go and West Ham's Bluey Wilkinson and Arthur Atkinson romped home to an easy victory, giving them a 6-1 and the match. There was pandemonium in the stadium and Mockford announced that he had to accept the decision for the time being. This statement incensed a section of the crowd even more and a group of about thirty supporters broke in to the Pavilion and demanded the blood of their own manager for giving in. Order was only restored when Mockford made a further announcement that he had already put in an official protest. The steward's excuse for allowing the race to continue was that from his position in the rostrum he could not see the tapes properly and was unaware that one was loose and caught round Newton's neck.

The re-run didn't do Crystal Palace any good as they lost again, this time by the even narrower score of 32-31.

After his success in introducing the starting gate, Mockford pioneered another innovation, this time electric timing. Sheffield had been employing this for some time, but the method employed by Crystal Palace was to be automatic in operation with the watch being started by the movement of the starting gate and the competitors stopping it by passing through a beam of light at the end of the race. It was hoped that this would give times to two decimal places and therefore be more accurate. The first meeting in which this was used was on 9 September in the league match against Coventry, which the Glaziers won by 32 points to 30, with Johnson scoring a maximum. Times throughout the meeting were taken by both the old and the new methods and there was never more than 0.2-second difference between them.

Following an unexpected away defeat at Wimbledon, Crystal Palace's chance of taking the league title disappeared. They were now out of the running in all three team competitions, but individually, they were just about to take the speedway world by storm.

The final of the Star Riders' Championship was held on 14 September at Wembley's Empire Stadium. Twenty of the best riders in speedway, two from each National League team, lined up for this prestigious event, the equivalent of the World Championship. Crystal Palace's representatives were Ron Johnson and Tom Farndon. Both won through their first round heats with some ease. Farndon then beat Les Wootton and Harry Whitfield in the first semi-final, while Johnson also won his semi-final, beating Phil Bishop and Walter Moore. Both therefore qualified for the final along with West Ham's Australian star, Bluey Wilkinson. As the tapes went up, Farndon and Wilkinson shot into the first bend together and for two laps the two fought it out neck and neck. As they crossed the line at the end of the second lap, Farndon slowly but surely began to assert his authority and gradually pulled away to become the Star Riders' champion for 1933. Behind him, Wilkinson had some bad luck when he lost his tyre and was overtaken by Johnson, giving Crystal Palace a 1-2 in the event.

Many commentators said after the meeting that this was definitely the best ever Star Riders' final and probably the most exciting meeting ever to take place at Wembley. Farndon thoroughly deserved his victory and Johnson reaffirmed his real championship class. Farndon had been threatening to break through into the realms of speedway superstardom all season, and now he had well and truly arrived. His victory was due to a combination of three factors: he started faster than anyone else; he was faster during the race than anyone else; and his control of the bike throughout was superb. He never once looked to be in any trouble.

Farndon proved his class in the Glaziers' next meeting when he was instrumental in the team's sterling victory over league champions, Wembley, by 42 points to 21, scoring a faultless maximum.

When the starting gate was introduced some pundits expressed the opinion that the riders would find a way round the improved system. Sure enough, it was now becoming more and more noticeable that most of the riders were getting wise to the habit of the starter. The current rule meant that the tapes were only lowered as the riders were at the line. Most starters were anxious to avoid broken tapes so they were raising the tape almost as soon as they were lowered. Knowing this, riders were now edging forward as soon as the tapes came down, letting in the clutch a split-second later. In one race in the match against Wembley, all four riders shot forward before the tapes had risen and had to duck underneath. To get round this, the Control Board introduced a new rule which said that the tapes were to be lowered before the riders reached the line.

Crystal Palace followed up their win over Wembley with a double over Plymouth, 41-22 at home and 32-30 away. Francis scored a maximum in both matches.

A collection of Crystal Palace badges together with those of local motor cycle clubs.

By now, however, Crystal Palace were well and truly out of contention for league honours and two late season defeats away at Clapton and home to Belle Vue meant they even lost out on the runners-up spot, finishing in fourth position.

Although it was a bit of a disappointing year for the team after the high hopes at the beginning, they could point to the fact that Farndon and Johnson had finished first and second in the Star Riders' Championship and that Johnson had been the Individual Match Race Champion, although towards the end of the season he lost the title to West Ham's Tiger Stevenson. Farndon also finished the season in sixth place in the averages with a C.M.A. of 9.56, having recorded nine full and one paid maximum. After a fairly average start to the season, Fardon's after the Star Rider's Final was nothing short of stunning, scoring five of his nine maximums between 11 September and 7 October in just seven matches. Johnson was in fifteenth place with 8.54, and not far behind him was Joe Francis on 8.19. He had scored six full and three paid maximums and had come right back into the form he shown in his earlier days, which had been somewhat missing over the last two or three years. After his return following the dispute with the Control Board, Nobby

A contemporary hand-drawn picture of the 1933 Crystal Palace team by young fan, Don Gray.

Key had not shown the same form as the previous year, and his average dropped two points to 6.79.

However, although it was now coming up to the end of the season, there was some sensational news still to come from promoters, Mockford and Smith. Visitor numbers to the Crystal Palace grounds were in general decline, and the only two attractions that were still regularly pulling in large numbers were the path racing and the speedway. The trustees of the Palace felt they needed to make their money out of these and consequently proposed a dramatic increase in rent to something like £1,000 per week. This, combined with their continued refusal to sanction floodlights at the speedway track, forced the promoters to seriously consider their future at Sydenham; on 13 October, it was announced that Messrs Mockford and Smith had completed negotiations to lay down a track at New Cross Stadium, and would transfer their operation there at the start of the 1934 season.

In a statement, the promoters said, 'Plans have been completed for the construction of a track that will be about 300 yards in circumference and unique in being the only small track banked all round. For the first time a tarmac foundation will be used which is expected to eliminate the possibilities of any bumps arising. New Cross is a modern stadium with up-to-date accommodation giving a close and uninterrupted view of the racing to every spectator. The meetings will be held at night and the most modern flood lighting equipment that it is possible to obtain will be installed. Fully equipped workshops are being installed and the work of laying the track will be put in hand at once, while the circuit will be open for practice immediately upon completion.'

The last meeting to take place at Crystal Palace for the time being – and the last ever in the senior sphere – was on 14 October when the Glaziers raced their rearranged fixture with West Ham and also took on and beat Clapton 32-29. In the second half a special handicap challenge match race was held between Tom Farndon and his manager, Fred Mockford. Mockford received a lap start and won by four lengths.

Following the meeting, the traditional end of season dance brought to an end the sixth season of racing at Crystal Palace. For the supporters it was now a case of goodbye Crystal Palace, hello New Cross.

1933 – National League

2 May	A	West Ham	L	24-36
6 May	H	West Ham	W	41-21
11 May	A	Wembley	L	24-39
13 May	H	Wimbledon	W	42-21
18 May	A	Nottingham	W	38-24
20 May	H	Sheffield	W	49-11
27 May	A	Clapton	L	21-37
27 May	H	Clapton	W	40-20
30 May	A	Plymouth	L	30-33
3 June	H	Coventry	W	44-18
5 June	A	Belle Vue	L	14-45
10 June	H	Belle Vue	W	37-26
15 June	A	Coventry	L	29-33
17 June	H	Nottingham	W	41-22
19 June	A	Wimbledon	L	29-33
24 June	H	Wembley	W	39-23

28 June	A	Sheffield	W	40-23
1 July	H	Plymouth	W	45-17
11 July	A	West Ham	W	37-26
15 July	H	Sheffield	W	32-31
7 August	A	Belle Vue	L	30-33
10 August	A	Coventry	W	34-26*
12 August	H	Nottingham	W	37-25
23 August	A	Sheffield	L	41-22
26 August	H	Wimbledon	W	46-17
7 September	A	Nottingham	L	32-31
9 September	H	Coventry	W	32-30
11 September	A	Wimbledon	L	29-34
16 September	H	Wembley	W	42-21
21 September	A	Wembley	L	27-35
30 September	H	Plymouth	W	41-22
3 October	A	Plymouth	W	32-30
7 October	A	Clapton	L	30-33
7 October	H	Belle Vue	L	30-33
14 October	H	West Ham	L	30-31
14 October	H	Clapton	W	32-29

*original score 36-24. Two points were deducted from Crystal Palace for George Newton using an oversized tyre.

National Trophy

Preliminary round
Bye

First round

18 July	A	West Ham	W	69-55
27 July	H	West Ham	D	63-63

Won 132-118 on aggregate

Semi final

17 August	A	Wembley	L	48-77
19 August	H	Wembley	L	62-63

Lost 110-140 on aggregate

London Cup

First round

| 3 July | A | Wimbledon | W | 65-60 |
| 8 July | H | Wimbledon | L | 49-77 |

Lost 114-137 on aggregate

Rider	M	R	Pts	BP	T	CMA	FM	PM
Tom Farndon	34	100	232	7	239	9.56	9	1
Ron Johnson	35	103	194	26	220	8.54	3	2
Joe Francis	36	106	206	11	217	8.19	6	3
Nobby Key	30	86	127	19	146	6.79	1	2
Harry Shepherd	36	108	126	22	148	5.48	2	1
George Newton	29	82	77	16	93	4.54	0	0
Lew Lancaster	11	22	16	2	18	3.27	0	0
Jack Jackson	8	12	8	1	9	3.00	0	0

Chapter Three

1934-1940

1934-1936

Following Mockford and Smith's departure, the Crystal Palace trustees themselves made efforts to continue path racing, and a few meetings were held at the end of 1933 and 1934, but by 1935 motorcycle racing in all its forms had come to an end at Crystal Palace. Then, quite out of the blue, towards the end of April 1936, the Crystal Palace management announced that they intended to reopen the old speedway track for training purposes.

Former favourite and Glaziers captain, Triss Sharp, was appointed as supervisor, and within a month, 150 applications had been received from novices wishing to use the facilities. Practice sessions were arranged for Saturday 23 May (2:00 p.m. to 6:00 p.m.) and Monday 25 May (4:30 p.m. to 6:30 p.m.). Of those invited to attend it was agreed that the most promising sixteen would be chosen to take part in a knock-out competition, which would be advertised as one of the Palace's Whit Monday attractions at 6:00 p.m. on 1 June.

The meeting was a big success and a further meeting was held on 3 August, the August bank holiday. This time the leading novice was West Ham's latest find, Lloyd Goffe, who later went on to have a very successful career with Wimbledon and Harringay after the Second World War, qualifying for one World Championship Final in 1949.

1937-1940

Crystal Palace continued to hold novice practice and bank holiday meetings throughout 1937 and 1938. Then, at the beginning of 1939, another surprise

Charlie Appleby receiving the trophy for winning the 1937 Whit Monday Novices' event.

announcement was made: after a gap of six years, the Glaziers would return to league racing. The promoters were the Palace trustees themselves, under the chairmanship of Sir Henry Buckland, while Sydney Legg, an employee of Crystal Palace, was to act as team manager. Sir Henry had always been very keen on speedway and in the 1928-33 period, was often seen top-hatted and immaculately dressed, striding round the centre green, making sure everything was running smoothly. Sydney Legg had also been associated with the earlier league meetings and had been the organiser of the 1936-38 open meetings.

Probably very wisely, they decided not to enter the top tier this time, but to start in the second division. At first no riders were announced as the new management decided to hold practice sessions and sign up the most promising newcomers. These were held every Saturday throughout March. This open invitation brought dozens of youngsters to the track to try out for the team. There was a feeling that Crystal Palace, with its wide open spaces, was probably the easiest track in the country to ride, and therefore just right for novices to learn their craft.

Although, of course, this idea of training up their own youngsters was very laudable, Crystal Palace did receive some criticism in the speedway press and from older hands that this policy could ultimately lead to disaster as, without at least one or two experienced riders, they would just get hammered week after week.

Their first encounter of the new era was a challenge match against Hackney Cubs on Easter Monday. The management responded to the criticism by bringing in an old hand, the South African Keith Harvey, to bolster the team. As it turned out, however, he was not really needed and scored just three points from one race as the Glaziers beat the Cubs 41-31, with the youngsters coming up trumps; Ernie Pawson scored a 12-point maximum and Mick Mitchell 9 paid 10 while Les Trim added 5 from two races. The rest of the team were Geo Gower (5 points), Andy Markham (4) and George Liddle (3).

Pawson and Mitchell surprised many of the critics with their superb performances. Pawson had, in fact, been around the speedways for three

Experienced South African rider, Keith Harvey, was brought into the 1939 Crystal Palace team to bolster up a team of juniors and novices.

years and had had his early training at Dagenham. He was on Harringay's books as a novice but had not managed to break into the team; until that first meeting at Crystal Palace, no one had really taken much notice of him. His faultless maximum came as something of a revelation. He was a foot-forward man and his style was ideal for the wide open spaces of Crystal Palace. He was also an expert mechanic and looked after his own motors.

The 25-year-old Mitchell, on the other hand, was an unashamed leg-trailer. He was reminiscent in style to the old Palace hero, Tom Farndon, with his leg well back, machine laid right over, ready to dash into any gap left by the riders in front.

And so the scene was set for a confident Crystal Palace outfit to race their first proper league match in six years. A new competition had been introduced into the Second Division for the 1939 season, the English Speedway Trophy, run on league lines, so it was this competition that saw the Glaziers' first official fixture of the season: an away fixture against Hackney Wick on 15 April. But away from the comfort of their own track, the young squad struggled, going down 57-27 to a rampant Hackney team. Only Harvey, Mitchell and Trim were really able to live with the Wolves, although a newcomer, Harold Saunders, showed some promise, scoring 4 points and pushing the Hackney skipper, Frank Hodgson, to a close decision in heat ten in the best race of the night. It was a salutary wake-up call after the euphoria of their opening victory.

Among the spectators in the Glaziers' first official league fixture at home was the man many thought responsible for bringing speedway to the Palace in the first place, Lionel Wills, now the head of a large Australian shipping concern. Just as the very first meeting had been ushered in by a heavy thunderstorm, so this one too started with a heavy rain shower and strong winds which blew the speakers in the middle of the centre green right round.

Lionel Wills wasn't the only old face to be seen that day; former Glazier Harry Shepherd lined up for the visiting Bristol team. Sadly, it was not to be a triumphant return to league racing as Crystal Palace went down 33-46. Once again it was Harvey, Mitchell and Trim, together with Pawson, who carried the fight to Bristol, but it was not enough as the rest of the youngsters struggled, even on their home track.

Although it was a loss, things were not quite as bad as the score suggested. For example, heat thirteen could have gone very differently. Andy Markham was excluded for jumping the start and the race developed into a battle between Mitchell and Bristol's Jack Bibby, but Bibby's engine started to play up and he dropped behind. Meanwhile, Bristol's other rider, Bill Melluish, had engine failure leaving Mitchell and Crystal Palace with what looked like a certain 3 points, even with Markham's exclusion. But then, at the end of the third lap, Mitchell's bike shed its chain, leaving Bibby to splutter on alone. Mitchell put up a heroic struggle to push his bike home for 2 points, but after getting to the fourth bend he collapsed with the effort, leaving the score 3-0 to Bristol instead of what might have been a 3-3, or even a 4-2 to the Palace if Markham had not breached the tapes.

So, in spite of starting the English Speedway Trophy with two defeats, the Crystal Palace management was still not too worried about its team of youngsters as they headed off for their third encounter, a return match with Bristol. At the end of heat five, the score was Bristol 15 Crystal Palace 14, but that was as good as it got for the Glaziers, as from then on Bristol ran away with the match finishing up victors by 51 points to 32. Once again it was Harvey and Mitchell and, to a lesser extent, Pawson and Trim who carried the team, the other four scoring just 3 points between them.

For the next match at home, Crystal Palace brought in two new juniors in the hope of strengthening the team, but it was not to be as Norwich triumphed 46-38. Harvey scored a maximum, while his partner, Les Trim, followed him home in two of their rides together and won his other race to finish with 8 paid 10. But with Mitchell and Pawson both having a poor day, there was no-one to back them up. Of the two newcomers, Vic Weir looked to be the most promising prospect as he managed 3 points from his two rides and went on to win his heat of the second half scratch race competition. Unfortunately, it was difficult to judge what sort of prospect the other junior, Charlie Challis, was likely to be, as he only managed to complete a grand total of one lap, suffering from engine failures in all five of his races.

The following week's match saw the start of their actual league campaign in a National League Second Division match against Middlesbrough. Although they lost once again, the Glaziers should really have won, but their machinery let them down badly. In two heats neither of the Glaziers finished at all. In another only one finished, but even his engine had failed and he just drifted home in third place. Mitchell did not finish one race, packing up in three and not coming out at all for his fourth, while Pawson's engine blew up and completely disintegrated. A new rider was brought into the team, Bronco Slade, but his carburettor fell to pieces so he was only able to contribute 1 point.

The one bright spot in the 39-43 defeat was the form of Vic Weir, who won his first scheduled ride in heat four and was then forced to ride in the last three heats due to the unavailability of machines for the rest of the team. He won them all, including a victory over Aub Lawson, who was on loan to

Middlesborough. Weir's main support was Keith Harvey, who won the three races he finished.

After the initial win over Hackney Cubs in a challenge match, the season had not gone well for the Glaziers, and it was about to get even worse. The team were annihilated 61-23 at Middlesbrough and then suffered their fourth consecutive home defeat, 39-43, at the hands of Bluey Wilkinson's Sheffield outfit. Another poor performance at Bristol, going down 83-22 in the National Trophy first round first leg, followed by their heaviest home defeat so far, 35-65 in the second leg, meant they were now bottom of both leagues with no points to their name and were out of the National Trophy after the first round. It was a worrying time for the Crystal Palace management who had pinned such great hope on their team of juniors led by the experienced Keith Harvey.

Sydney Legg decided the time was right to bring in two new riders to help bolster the team. The two he signed up were George Dykes from Leeds and West Ham's Eddie Barker. Barker was a colourful character, a Canadian by birth, and known as 'Flash' Barker. The nickname Flash came from his resemblance to the comic book hero, Flash Gordon. His other claim to fame was that he was also a well-known all-in wrestler, known in the ring as Ed (Blondie) Gordon.

With these two signed up, Crystal Palace's next match was a home English Trophy encounter against Hackney Wick. With one heat to go, Palace were 1 point behind, and another defeat looked on the cards. Mitchell gated first but the Hackney pair of Geo Saunders and Jim Baylais cleverly shut Keith Harvey out. Harvey, meanwhile, just wound everything on and eventually managed to pass the Hackney pair round the outside in one deft move. The relief at seeing the home side come home with a 5-1 and the match was palpable; the big Whit Monday crowd darkened the air by throwing their hats, programmes and anything else they could get their hands on, up in jubilation. After their poor run it was a magnificent last heat victory. The heroes of the day were once again Harvey with 10 paid 11, Mitchell 10 and Weir with 7 paid 9. With his bikes now being looked after by former New Cross mechanic, Strudwick, Charlie Challis also rode well for his 7 points. Legg felt able to tell the fans that 'the tide has turned. Now that we have our first win the boys will pull together much better.'

Sadly, things were not to turn out that way. The Glaziers were once again thumped in their next match, an away fixture at Newcastle. Going down 58-25, only Mitchell put up any sort of show with 8 points from three completed rides. Even Harvey only managed 1 point this time. Still worse was to come; in their next match, Crystal Palace lost 62-20 away at Stoke. Once again Mitchell was the only one of the Glaziers to trouble the Stoke boys.

1939 team member, Ed 'Flash' Barker, was also a professional wrestler, operating under the name, Ed 'Blondie' Gordon.

With two bad away defeats following Mr Legg's statement that 'things could only get better', much now depended on the next home fixture against Sheffield. The scores remained close throughout the match, but going into the last heat, the Glaziers needed a 5-1 to score their second much-needed victory. With Mitchell and Harvey lined up against Paddy Mills and Aussie Powell, the home crowd still believed it could be done.

As the gate flew up, Mitchell and Harvey shot into the lead and stayed level making it almost impossible for the Sheffield pair to get past, but on the third corner, Harvey hit a bump and fell. Mills, immediately behind him, laid his bike down to avoid the fallen rider. The race was stopped immediately and an announcement was made that the race would be restarted with the exclusion of Aussie Powell. Since Powell had not been anywhere near Harvey at the time he fell, the whole stadium was mystified. After about a minute or so, a correction was made and that it was Harvey who was, quite rightly, excluded. What this meant to the match result was that Crystal Palace could now only win if Mitchell finished alone, an extremely unlikely scenario as the two Sheffield riders could let him go and just make sure they finished. However, Mills hit a bump coming off the second bend and once again the race was stopped with this time Mills being excluded from the rerun. At the third time of asking, Powell decided against heroics and tootled round finishing half a lap behind Mitchell, but his two points gave victory to Sheffield by the narrowest of margins, 41-40, and brought Crystal Palace's optimism that they had turned the corner to a final juddering halt.

The following week saw a brief respite for Crystal Palace as the World Championship first-round heats were held. Aub Lawson won the Palace round with a 15-point maximum. Mitchell and Challis were the home team's best, both scoring seven points.

But it was back to the same old story the following week as the Glaziers took on and lost to Bristol 37-46 at home. All three of their top riders – Harvey, Mitchell and Weir – failed to finish in two of their races, either through falls or engine failures, and it was left to yet another new import, Bob Lovell, to carry the fight to Bristol with 9 points. Two other newcomers were brought into the team for the match – Ron Clarke and Charlie Appleby – but neither made much of an impact.

There was now a good deal of anxiety inside the Crystal Palace management. The poor form of the team was seen as a major reason for the alarming drop in attendances. Middlesbrough had just closed through lack of support and there was great concern that the Glaziers would soon go the same way if things didn't improve on the track. But things were about to get even worse as the Glaziers were crushed 63-21 by Sheffield. Ten of the fourteen heats resulted in 5-1s to Sheffield. There were no redeeming features for Crystal Palace as they suffered their heaviest league defeat of the season.

Finally, the moment came when the whole of the Crystal Palace team, free from engine failures and other misfortunes, all clicked at the same time. The next home match, on 24 June, resulted in a 56-28 destruction of Stoke. Leading the charge were Mitchell and Weir with paid maximums, backed up strongly by Harvey, Lovell, Clarke, Appleby, Challis and Trim. Even the luck seemed to be with the Glaziers this time as in heat thirteen, Appleby fell at the start, rolled over onto his feet, pulled his fallen machine up, restarted and then managed to fight his way through to second place.

Sadly, this overwhelming victory was watched by very few people as most had now given up on their team. After one more match – a loss away at Norwich (50-34) on 1 July – the Crystal Palace management decided that enough was enough and withdrew the team from the league. Although there were 1,100 members of the supporters' club, most meetings had been run at a big loss, sometimes as much as £100 per match, the equivalent of something like £3,000 in today's money. Many pundits felt that the main problem was the management's continued refusal to pay for floodlighting, a key factor that had led to Crystal Palace's closure back in 1933. Speedway meetings held in the afternoon rarely attracted the same sort of attendances as those held in the evening. 40,000 spectators had turned out for the first meeting of the season, very few of those turned out for the last.

But it wasn't quite the end of speedway at Crystal Palace, as three more meetings were held before the final curtain came down. Later in 1939, when an individual trophy called The Holiday Cup was held on August Bank Holiday as part of the day's festivities at the Palace, a number of the 1939 team turned out including Les Trim, Charlie Appleby, Charlie Page and George Liddle. But the meeting was won by West Ham's Colin Watson from Phil Bishop and Archie Windmill.

Upon the outbreak of the Second World War, all speedway in Great Britain was suspended, but there were a few wartime meetings held, most notably at Belle Vue who managed to run throughout the war period, and Rye House who only missed 1944. Several other tracks managed to hold one or two meetings, and one of these was Crystal Palace who put on two Holiday Cup meetings in 1940 at Easter and Whitsun. For the first time since the Palace closed in 1933, some big names were back in action at these two meetings. The Easter meeting saw West Ham's Arthur Atkinson (one of the favourites for the 1939 World Championship final, which was never held) beat team-mate Colin Watson in the final, with Keith Harvey third. Tiger Stevenson and Wally Lloyd were other star names to appear. But in spite of these big names,

The programme for Crystal Palace's last-ever home fixture, a second division match against Stoke held on 24 June 1939.

CRYSTAL PALACE

General Manager - SIR HENRY BUCKLAND

Programme—AUGUST BANK HOLIDAY, 1939

TERRACE BANDSTAND

From 11.30 a.m. NON-STOP VARIETY.

SPEEDWAY

2 to 2.30. DRUMS AND FIFES OF H.M. 2ND BATT. THE ROYAL WARWICKSHIRE REGIMENT.

2.30 **MOTOR-CYCLE RODEO**

AFTER RODEO (About 4 o'clock)

GRAND DISPLAY OF BROCK'S DAYLIGHT FIREWORKS

5.30 to 6 DRUMS AND FIFES OF H.M. 2ND BATT. THE ROYAL WARWICKSHIRE REGIMENT

6 p.m. **MOTOR-CYCLE SPEEDWAY RACING**

SPORTS GROUND

3 to 3.30. DRUMS AND FIFES OF H.M. 2ND BATT. THE ROYAL WARWICKSHIRE REGIMENT

3.30 **GREAT OPEN-AIR BOXING TOURNAMENT**

NORTH TOWER GARDENS

11.30 to 2

3.30 to 5.30 } CRYSTAL PALACE BAND.

6 to 8

PLEASURE FAIR

From 10 a.m. ROUNDABOUTS, SWINGS AND VARIOUS AMUSEMENTS

CENTRE FOUNTAIN

6.30 to 7. DRUMS AND FIFES OF H.M. 2ND BATT. THE ROYAL WARWICKSHIRE REGIMENT.

FIRST AID

Ladies of the St. John Ambulance Brigade are in attendance.
Their Depot is at the Centre Walk end of Sports Ground Stand.

PRICE : THREEPENCE

The programme cover for the 1939 August Bank Holiday meeting.

it was former Crystal Palace rider, Keith Harvey, who set the fastest time of the night with a new track record of 79.8 seconds.

The Whitsun meeting, held on 13 May, was won by Hackney's Phil 'Tiger' Hart, but the biggest cheer of the night came when former Glaziers' captain, Ron Johnson, took to the track. Unfortunately he was leading the final when he suffered a puncture and had to withdraw. This race, in which the second and third riders were Archie Windmill and Fred Tuck, was the last ever to be held at Crystal Palace. Speedway did not resume at the Palace after the War, though not for the want of trying. In 1948 and again in 1950, Croydon Speedways Ltd tried to get permission to use the old track, but each time local residents protested to the council about noise levels and the council refused permission.

The old track has long since disappeared and the site of the old wooden stands is now covered by the Crystal Palace National Sports Centre Athletics Track grandstand.

1939 – National League Division Two

6 May	H	Middlesborough	L	39-43
12 May	A	Middlesborough	L	23-61
13 May	H	Sheffield	L	39-43
1 June	A	Stoke	L	20-62
3 June	H	Sheffield	L	40-41
5 June	A	Newcastle	L	25-58
17 June	H	Bristol	L	37-46
22 June	A	Sheffield	L	21-63
24 June	H	Stoke	W	56-28
1 July	A	Norwich	L	34-50

English Speedway Trophy

15 April	A	Hackney Wick	L	27-57
22 April	H	Bristol	L	33-46
25 April	A	Bristol	L	32-51
29 April	H	Norwich	L	35-46
20 May	A	Norwich	L	20-64
29 May	H	Hackney Wick	W	43-40

SPEEDWAY RACING

AT 6 P.M.   **PAVILION 2/-**   **STAND SEATS 6d.**

Organised by the Crystal Palace Management under the Speedway Regulations of the Auto-Cycle Union.
A.C.U. Track Licence No. 285. Permit No. T.A. 1,062. All races over 4 laps (1,796 yards). Clutch start.
4-Lap Clutch Start Track Record: 79.8 secs.=46.03 m.p.h., established by Keith Harvey, 25/3/40.
A.C.U. Steward in Charge of Meeting: Mr. A. W. Day. *A.C.U. Judge-Timekeeper:* Mr. J. W. Barber.
BETTING STRICTLY PROHIBITED

INDIVIDUAL CONTEST FOR

THE HOLIDAY CUP

Points in Each Race:—First, Three; Second, Two; Third, One

(NOTE.—The eight highest-point scorers in the 12 heats will take part in semi-finals.)

RIDERS:

R. C. APPLEBY	P. M. HART	RON JOHNSON	LESLIE TRIM
KEN BRETT	KEITH HARVEY	JEFFREY LLOYD	FRED TUCK
GEO. CRAIG	BOB HALL	WALLY LLOYD	VIC. WEIR
ALEX. GRAY	RON HOWES	MICK MITCHELL	A. A. WINDMILL

Event	Colour	Rider	Result	Points
HEAT 1 ...	Red ...	R. C. APPLEBY	1st	3
Time	Blue ...	KEN BRETT ...	2nd	2
	White ...	ALEX. GRAY	3rd	1
	Yellow ...	BOB HALL		
HEAT 2 ...	Red ...	RON HOWES	1st	3
Time	Blue ...	JEFFREY LLOYD ...	2nd	2
	White ...	A. A. WINDMILL ...		
	Yellow ...	VIC. WEIR ...	3rd	1
HEAT 3 ...	Red ...	FRED TUCK ...	1st	3
Time	Blue ...	MICK MITCHELL ...	2nd	2
	White ...	GEO. CRAIG ...		
	Yellow ...	LESLIE TRIM ...	3rd	1
HEAT 4 ...	Red ...	KEITH HARVEY ...	1st	3
Time	Blue ...	RON JOHNSON ...	2nd	2
	White ...	P. M. HART		
	Yellow ...	WALLY LLOYD ...	3rd	1
HEAT 5 ...	Red ...	RON HOWES ...	1st	3
Time	Blue ...	KEN BRETT ...	2nd	2
	White ...	GEO. CRAIG ...		
	Yellow ...	WALLY LLOYD ...	3rd	1
HEAT 6 ...	Red ...	R. C. APPLEBY ...	1st	3
Time	Blue ...	JEFFREY LLOYD ...	2nd	2
	White ...	P. M. HART ...		
	Yellow ...	LESLIE TRIM ...	3rd	1
HEAT 7 ...	Red ...	FRED TUCK ...	1st	3
Time	Blue ...	RON JOHNSON ...	2nd	2
	White ...	ALEX. GRAY ...		
	Yellow ...	A. A. WINDMILL	3rd	1
HEAT 8 ...	Red ...	KEITH HARVEY ...	1st	3
Time	Blue ...	MICK MITCHELL ...	2nd	2
	White ...	VIC. WEIR ...		
	Yellow ...	BOB HALL ...	3rd	1
HEAT 9 ...	Red ...	RON JOHNSON ...	1st	3
Time	Blue ...	KEN BRETT ...	2nd	2
	White ...	VIC. WEIR ...		
	Yellow ...	LESLIE TRIM ...	3rd	1

Above and next page: Results sheets from last-ever Crystal Palace programme held on 13 May 1940.

Event	Colour	Rider	Result	Points
HEAT 10 ...	Red ...	R. C. APPLEBY	1st	3
Time	Blue ...	KEITH HARVEY ...	2nd	2
	White ...	GEO. CRAIG	3rd	1
	Yellow ...	A. A. WINDMILL		
HEAT 11 ...	Red ...	MICK MITCHELL ...	1st	3
Time	Blue ...	JEFFREY LLOYD ...	2nd	2
	White ...	ALEX. GRAY ...	3rd	1
	Yellow ...	WALLY LLOYD ...		
HEAT 12 ...	Red ...	RON HOWES ...	1st	3
Time	Blue ...	FRED TUCK	2nd	2
	White ...	P. M. HART	3rd	1
	Yellow ...	BOB HALL		

RIDERS' SCORE CHART

NAME	1st	2nd	3rd	TOTAL
R. C. APPLEBY STEVE LAWCTON	3		2	4
KEN BRETT			0	4
GEO. CRAIG	1			4
ALEX. GRAY	1			4
P. M. HART	3		2	4
KEITH HARVEY				
BOB HALL				
RON HOWES				
RON JOHNSON GEORGE GOWER	1	3	2	6
JEFFREY LLOYD CHARLIE PAGE				
WALLY LLOYD				
MICK MITCHELL				
LESLIE TRIM		2		5
FRED TUCK				
VIC. WEIR				
A. A. WINDMILL		2	3	

FIRST SEMI-FINAL

Red ......
Blue ......
White ......
Yellow ......   WINNER ...... *Johnson*

Time ......

SECOND SEMI-FINAL

Red ......
Blue ......
White ......
Yellow ......   WINNER ...... *Phil*

Time 86 8

FINAL

Red (1st in 1st Semi-Final) ......   RETD PUNCTURE WHEN 1ST
Blue (2nd in 1st Semi-Final) 2ND
White (1st in 2nd Semi-Final) 1ST
Yellow (2nd in 2nd Semi-Final) 3RD

WINNER ......   Time ......

Phil 'Tiger' Hart, third from right, winner of Crystal Palace's last meeting, shown here in the Crystal Palace paddock.

National Trophy

First Round

16 May	A	Bristol	L	22-83
27 May	H	Bristol	L	35-65

Lost 57-148 on aggregate

National League Division Two

Rider	M	Pts	Ave
Bob Lovell	7	40	5.7
Vic Weir	10	56	5.6
Keith Harvey	10	53	5.3
Mick Mitchell	10	51	5.1
Ron Clarke	5	12	5.0
Les Trim	7	34	4.9
Ernie Pawson	3	13	4.3

Charlie Appleby	4	13	3.3
Charlie Challis	10	28	2.8
Charlie Page	2	5	2.5
Geo Gower	5	12	2.4
George Liddle	2	4	2.0
George Dykes	3	3	1.0
Austin Humphries	1	1	1.0
Bronco Slade	1	1	1.0

English Speedway Trophy

Rider	M	Pts	Ave
Keith Harvey	6	50	8.3
Mick Mitchell	6	32	5.3
Les Trim	6	32	5.3
Ernie Pawson	5	23	4.6
Vic Weir	3	13	4.3
Harry Saunders	2	7	3.5
George Dykes	2	6	3.0
Charlie Challis	3	7	2.3
Andy Markham	4	7	1.8
George Liddle	3	5	1.7
Eddie Barker	2	3	1.5
Geo Gower	5	5	1.0
Fred Wiseman	1	0	0.0

Conclusion

Crystal Palace Speedway was born in the age of speed when humans were pushing the boundaries as never before. The early meetings at High Beech had brought a whole new exciting and exhilarating sport to the British public and they loved it. Over the next couple of years, dozens of tracks opened all around the country as people flocked to see the leather-clad warriors tearing round the track, seemingly defying death at every turn.

One of the earliest of these new tracks was Crystal Palace, the second to open in London, just three months after the first meeting. The racing was some of the best in the country and it brought to the public heroes such as Triss Sharp, Ron Johnson and Tom Farndon. In the early 1930s, Crystal Palace was on top of the world attracting crowds of 20 or 30,000 through the turnstiles regularly every week.

Sadly however, the management of the Crystal Palace itself never fully understood speedway crowds and what made the racing so exciting; they saw it as just another money-making attraction. Their refusal to install floodlights to allow evening racing and their proposal to increase the rent led the promoters, Fred Mockford and Cecil Smith, to say 'enough is enough'. They moved operations to a new purpose-built track.

Crystal Palace's own attempts at staging speedway in the latter years of the 1930s was a disaster, and so the track that had once attracted tens of thousands and been acknowledged as one of the best in the country closed down, never to reopen. When the real speedway boom set in after the Second World War, Crystal Palace was in no position to take part. Precious relics such as badges and programmes and the fading memories of an ever-dwindling number of fans who actually saw racing at Crystal Palace are now all we have left to remind us of the glory years at what was once one of speedway's premier tracks.